Lambeth to Lamsdorf:
Doug Hawkins' War

Robin Green

Published by

**MELROSE
BOOKS**

An Imprint of Melrose Press Limited
St Thomas Place, Ely
Cambridgeshire
CB7 4GG, UK
www.melrosebooks.co.uk

FIRST EDITION

Copyright © Robin Green 2015

The Author asserts his moral right to
be identified as the author of this work

Cover designed by Melrose Books

ISBN 978-1-910792-14-8

Printed and bound in Great Britain by:
CPI Group (UK) Ltd, Croydon, CR0 4YY

FSC
www.fsc.org
MIX
Paper from
responsible sources
FSC® C013604

Photograph of Dougie as a rookie at enlistment, aged 18

Foreword

In April 2009, I started to film interviews with Prisoners of War veterans on one of my biggest productions to date – 'The Long March to Freedom'. On the first morning of a two-week long shooting schedule, our first of 40 such interviews, we heard incredible stories of endurance, stamina and, above all, courage. We heard not only how they had survived the humiliation of capture and the four to five years in a Prisoner of War camp, but how they endured the almost three months of walking west, in the worse winter on record, away from the Russian advance. It has been estimated that over 300,000 such P.O.W.s suffered this ordeal on many marches right across the German homeland, which was of course Poland and Germany as we know it today.

We travelled to Basingstoke on our second morning's filming and met veteran Douglas Hawkins. Upon arriving at the house, this frail little man, in a red pullover, arrived at the door and welcomed us in, not knowing what was required of him. He offered us all drinks and, while he kindly made them, we set up our equipment. While drinking our tea and coffee we had a general chat and explained what we wanted from him in the way of telling his extraordinary story. He was extremely excited, but nervous at the same time. We kept assuring him that although it was called an 'interview' we would in fact just be chatting. We wanted to know about his life in the army, from joining up, about his capture, his time in the German prison camp, and his journey home to freedom – the long walk across Germany.

As he started to tell us his amazing stories, his eyes would well up and tears would run down his face. I thought the film ordeal was getting to him and we stopped filming. "No," he insisted, "let's continue," and, once more after wiping his eyes on a clean handkerchief, we continued at a specific memory, his eyes would well up and tears would appear, but he insisted that we shouldn't stop. We continued like this during the two hours of filming, his handkerchief becoming completely soaked with tears.

He was a frail man, whose early life, which should have been one of enjoyment, had been extracted from him. Once he turned eighteen, conscription called him into the army. After his initial training he spent but a few months in action before he was captured. He was off to a prison camp with many others to live out the rest of the war. But then in the January of 1945 he, and many thousands like him, were forced to march west, away from the advancing aggressive Russian Army.

I felt sorry for Doug that his early life had been taken from him. Somehow, I felt an affinity with him, and from that interview we became friends as I discovered that we had both lived in the same hometown, Mitcham. During the interview, Doug spoke of the places and locations where I had spent my childhood. Weeks after the interview he continually rang me to tell more stories that he had forgotten.

The story of Doug's early life will give the reader an insight into and understanding of what many soldiers suffered in war, or as Doug puts it "90% boredom and 10% sheer terror."

The story of the Long March, or Death March, is a story that should never be forgotten. From Doug's own personal account of those experiences you can understand the extent of the treatment he and many others received at the hands of the Germans before he was finally reunited with his family.

I was proud to have met Doug and the many other veterans who appeared in the documentary, while at the same time satisfied that the three-part series, like Doug's own account in *Lambeth to Lamsdorf: Doug Hawkins' War*, will form part of a record of war that will never be forgotten.

Stephen Saunders – TV Producer, ASA Productions
October, 2013

Preface

This is not a story of beribboned Generals standing alone delivering accounts of their strategic successes or tactical nous, nor of historians eruditely expressing their opinion or counter-opinion of decisions, triumphs, failures or missed opportunities, told with hindsight. It is the story of an anonymous teenager, an apprentice welder, now 89-years-old who was engulfed by the uncontrollable and ruthless forces of circumstance.

There was no service manual that could prepare him for what he was to meet, witness and suffer. Nor was there any such manual from which some 300,000 others could benefit who found themselves in like circumstances. The camaraderie of a few friends, an inner determination and sheer bloody-minded stubbornness, as well as the innate belief that one day all this would end either in rescue or death maintained his hope. His is a story of humanity and inhumanity.

There have been few personal accounts written about the survivors of the 'Long March'. I have asked myself why this aspect of the last throes of the Second World War has been barely reported for 60 years. It was only in about 2005 that publications in book form appeared. Charles Waite's story, written by Dee de Vardera, and Richard Fuzniac's account of his father's experiences of a similar kind are the only two published accounts that I have encountered to date. Books, films, articles and reports abound about such exploits as the Great Escape, Colditz Castle, the Dam Busters and the D-Day Landings. Important as they are, only the D-Day Landings approach the scale in time and manpower of the little known 'Long March'.

"... this is an account of the dreary and miserable life endured by most Prisoners Of War (POWs) and of the terrible days of the march from Prussia (and Upper Silesia) to the West without food, medical support, proper clothing or shelter during one of the harshest winters in continental Europe of the 20th Century".[1]

This is a story that must be told and retold, for it has as much resonance today as it did in 1945. Doug Hawkins was one of many who survived. I count myself fortunate indeed to have first met him over ten years ago, and proud today to be privileged to recount his story for the benefit of a wider audience.

Robin Green (author)

---

[1] Hermann 22. 'Customer Reviews', Amazon Publishing

Dedication

This book is dedicated to Richard Sharman (London Defence Volunteer/Home Guard), John Auger (Private, Cheshire Regiment) and Frank Stapleton (Lance Corporal, Royal Engineers), the three good friends I lost too early in their life.

Contents

Illustrations and maps

Acknowledgements

I would like to thank and acknowledge the contributions of the following in the writing of the book:

1. Mrs J. Z. Chaddock, researcher, for following all the avenues to establish the historical evidence that underpins this narrative. Without her persistence and diligence this story could not have been written.

2. Mr Geoff Crump, archivist for the Chester Military Museum, whose assistance started me on the right track.

3. My wife, who has patiently appraised my drafts and whose suggestions have helped me to maintain my direction.

4. My daughter, Zoe, for patiently typing up the original manuscript.

5. The Cheshire Regiment Museum and its Curator, Major Pickering, for allowing me access to their Campaign Diaries and use of their archive material.

6. Ann Wicks, archivist, World War II Experience Centre, Wetherby, Yorkshire.

7. Mr Peter Hopkins, Publications Secretary, Merton Historical Society, for providing historical documentation from 1930 to 1950.

8. Stephen Saunders, ASA Productions, for his encouragement and support and the use of the transcript of his interviews with Dougie Hawkins.

9. Alan Bailey, for his checking of translations into German and from German.

Part One:
In the Beginning

March 27th 1924 was as special a day in the Hawkins' household in Somerleyton Road, Lambeth, as it was for me. It was the day I arrived, innocent, yelling and moist into this world, the newest arrival in the household now numbering ten.

We occupied the second and third floors of a substantial bay-fronted late Victorian terrace; a white collar worker's home of comfortable means. We lived above the Lorimers. They were a husband and wife, theatrical people, and two sons, Max and Alex. Max became the 'Cheeky Chappie' of 1930s musical hall known as Max Wall, a comedian and entertainer of the theatre, radio and later television. Max's earliest appearance on stage was aged two. His older brother was a talented musician who played guitar, ukulele and banjo. Together with my elder brother, Ron, they made novelty banjo- or ukulele-shaped cigar and cigarette boxes that could be tuned and played. They were sold in the smarter pubs and clubs of the West End of London, and Max and Alex became quite well known in this enterprise. Although much older than me, Max was a mischievous and amusing friend. As I recall, it was never dull when Max was around. As Max Wall grew older and pursued his livelihood in the theatre, I lost track of him. However, new friends and acquaintances took his place. School beckoned, new people were to fill my life, new goals to be achieved and new adventures to be had.

My father was a keen cricketer, a spin bowler of some repute. He passed on this interest and his bowling skills to me, which served me well throughout my life. Early skills were learnt playing street cricket. Windows were broken regularly, yet my father always paid for their replacement.

As the large Hawkins family grew up, the home we occupied in Somerleyton Road seemed to shrink, and so my parents took the decision to move on and purchased a larger home with a garden in which my father's growing interest in gardening could be given free rein. I was about eight when we settled into 5, Preshaw Crescent, Mitcham. This would be in about 1932.

My Junior School was next door to Brixton Police Station. This was in the days when the local Bobby knew his patch and everyone living there. He knew the honest and the scoundrel, the fair trader and the dodgy dealer. He dispensed justice with an avuncular approach, was fair, proportionate and well respected. Retribution could be swift and summary if caught 'nicking' an apple from a market barrow: a sharp clip across the ear would suffice for the miscreant. More serious transgressions, however, would probably be dealt with formally and take longer to resolve.

Where I learnt to play cricket, Somerleyton Road

A large street market used to stretch the length of Brixton Road. I believe it still does. It was a boisterous, colourful and exciting place to

2

be, and attracted people from far afield. One market trader I recall who always pitched his stall near to Brixton railway station sold nothing but toilet tissue from a handcart, or sometimes a cart pulled by a horse. His wares would be piled high, neatly stacked in columns on the bed of the cart. We derived much fun from discreetly pushing the cart or enticing the horse to move forward, so causing the stacked columns to topple and cascade onto the roadway. We awaited the predictable reaction of the stall holder. We were never disappointed when he raged at us scallywags as we gleefully darted away in all directions in order to avoid the grubby calloused palm of his hand warming our ears. Temptation is a delightful thing.

Kingston's was a fruit and vegetable retail shop near to the Police Station in Brixton Road. Of an evening, after it was closed for business we nine-, ten- and 11-year-olds had a fascination to discover how to retrieve apples from his display shelves inside the shop. We devised a plan. The locked green door to the shop had a long narrow ventilation slide that covered a similarly large rectangular-shaped opening in the door. This slide was always left in the open position to permit free flow of air across the fruit overnight.

Our strategy was to reach through this ventilator opening, armed with a long sharpened cane, which would reach to the displayed apples immediately opposite the door. Thereafter, it was easy to spear fruit and retrieve it through the opening. The team would work well together, one of us spearing and two keeping 'cave'. These learnt skills were to serve me well much later on in very different circumstances.

We were caught from time to time. Being close to the Brixton Police Station, we were subject to the vagaries of comings and goings of tall men in pointed conical hats. On one occasion, I recall, an authoritative voice demanded, "And what are you three up to?"

"Nothing, Sir," came the meek reply.

"Off home you lot, before I take you there myself."

We were gone in an instant. This was a close call, until next time!

Close to our home in Somerleyton Road lived two elderly ladies. They kept themselves to themselves, were respected and had probably seen hard times during the First World War. Indeed, our neighbour

Mrs Lorimer's nanny, known as Aunty Betty to us, was killed on 16th September 1916 by a bomb dropped from Zeppelin L31, one of the later bombing raids on London.

When boredom overtook our common sense we would find an opportunity to discreetly tie a string to our victims' front door knocker, and, whilst hiding behind the low front wall of the house, we would pull the string to rattle the knocker. When the knock was answered we would skedaddle, giggling with the vicarious thrill of having annoyed and disturbed our elderly victims. This is the sort of childish activity the author would sometimes indulge in on 'Mischief Night', that is, 4th November, the evening before 'Bonfire Night'. The Devil finds work for idle hands!

I have a vivid memory of 'Daddy Weston', a teacher whose philosophy told him that children should be seen and not heard, and woe betide any pupil who tested this belief. Daddy Weston was well known for administering instant justice. There was a group of what would loosely be described in the 1930s as 'gypsies' who lived in an area of Mitcham called 'Rocky'. One of the children from Rocky caught Daddy Weston's eye once too often. Daddy's response was a sharp physical chastisement. This proved to be a mistake, for the lad's father arrived at school the next day and dealt with Daddy Weston by means of a well-directed punch to the face. We cheered loudly at this spectacle. It was better than Roy Rogers and Gene Autry at a Saturday matinee. Such memories live a long time.

Terry Bull had a coal yard in Gladstone Road. As the coal men left to deliver and returned to reload their horse-drawn cart they would call out, "Coal man, Coal."

Mr Bull had a pet Mynah bird in his office, and on hearing the coal men's call it would reply with unrepeatable expletives. I wonder, who taught the bird?

I left school at 14 years to become apprenticed to a company that fabricated and engineered various items in metal. This firm was Corfields and Buckle, and it manufactured a variety of components for aircraft. My training was as an acetylene welder. It was not something that particularly took my fancy, but it would lead to a skill for which there would always be a demand with the prospect of war on the horizon. This was 1938.

There was a tradition in the family of service to the country in the Army. I had four elder brothers. My father and three of my brothers had all been together in the Territorial Army during the inter-war years. At the outbreak of war in September 1939, after the false hope of 'Peace in Our Time', all territorials were first in line for service. My eldest brother joined the Royal Artillery. Another became an engineer in the Royal Electrical and Mechanical Engineers, whilst one of my sisters worked in a munitions factory.

I had joined the Home Guard whilst still too young to contribute to the war effort in any other capacity. Subsequently, I was to meet the German equivalent of the Home Guard, but under very different circumstances. More of that later. I became a 'runner'; that is, a messenger who would be tasked to contact other senior Home Guard personnel in the event of an incident. This usually meant taking to my bicycle and haring around the streets in the blackout, knocking on doors to pass on my message. It is fortunate that cars were a rarity in 1940. My message was usually directed towards mustering all personnel to a rendezvous where a briefing would be carried out. The rendezvous was usually the golf club house on Mitcham Common. It had a bar and a snooker table, comfortable chairs and heating. It was well chosen.

This voluntary work was exciting for a teenager. I felt involved whilst having an armband (LDV) with a badge and a tin hat that set me apart. It was, however, no training for what was to come.

*57th Surrey (Mitcham) Battalion Home Guard. I am on the back row,
extreme right. Courtesy Merton Historical Society*

At this time, home was a happy place. There was always coming and
going, incessant chatter, plans being discussed, opinions aired, and the
warm cocooning of family life.

I recall I used to visit a cricket bat maker who had premises in High
Street, Sutton. He was Maurice Odd, of Odd and Son. I was about ten
or 12 at the time, and fascinated by the machinery, lathes and the like,
and by the various shaping tools that were used. "How do you get the
springs in the handle?" This was one of the mysteries explained to me.
Each bat would be tailor-made to the exact specification of the client.
Maurice was a skilled craftsman.

The toe of the bat always had a small conical-shaped depression on
it. I thought this was where you put the oil into the bat. My Dad had
always said that you had to keep the bat well oiled! With a kindly and
knowing smile Mr Odd explained that this was the hole made by the
lathe to grip it before being turned. The fascination of this workshop
never left me. The smell of willow sap and wood dust that pervaded
everywhere within the premises has stayed with me to this day.

Western Road Secondary School had been an enjoyable experience
and a happy place to be. Albeit no academic, I held my own in the bustle

of school life and even made my mark as more than a fair cricketer, thanks to my dad's coaching. I still possess two cricket match balls, each with engraved escutcheon; the reward for achieving a hat-trick of wickets on separate occasions, one of which was at the Harrogate County Ground, Yorkshire, with the test and Yorkshire batsman, Maurice Leyland, in attendance as team Captain.

My mother was a housewife and looked after us all very well. She must have been the busiest of us all in such a household. My father was a draughtsman in the construction industry.[2] This took him far afield, once to the Forth Bridge on an inspection, and on another occasion to Shoreham-on-Sea to inspect the new Top Secret 'Mulberry Docks' before their use on D-Day, June 1944.

So with my military connections, and already being a member of a quasi-military organisation, or perhaps, being christened after Lawrence of Arabia, I was destined to be drawn to the Services.

Mitcham Common was our preferred place from which to watch the pyrotechnics over London during the Blitz. Mitcham itself, although a long way from the strategically important docklands, received unwelcome aerial gifts courtesy of the Luftwaffe. At times, as elsewhere, it felt we were on the front line of the war in Mitcham. It was on one of these stray raids that my best friend from school, Richard Sharman, also in the Home Guard and a year older than me, was killed by a German landmine.

It was a curious incident, albeit a dramatic one, which had a far-reaching impact and deeply affected the community of which I was a part.

---

[2] Moorland and Haine.

The Tower Creamery, which took a direct hit on 16th April 1941, killing many members of the Home Guard

The plaque commemorating the fallen

Courtesy of the Merton Historical Society

On 16th April, 1941 it was reported that parachutes were seen descending near to Mitcham Common. To the lay onlookers this could only be an airborne assault. Thus it was so reported. Members of B Company 57th Surrey Home Guard, of which I was one, were on duty in the Tower Creameries. B Company members ran towards where the sightings had been reported. It transpired that the parachutes did not support soldiers but land mines. The massive explosion of the first landmine on Mitcham Common killed some of our men as they ran towards it. Others were killed in the explosion and fire that followed as a second landmine fell on the Tower Creamery. Fifteen of B Company lost their lives that night, among them Richard Sharman, my good friend from school days. He was 17. Richard was gone. It was the first time that I felt the deep emotions of loss. I really did not understand what had happened or why. This feeling of loss, however, was to become a recurring theme during the next five years.

Since then the Tower Creameries has been redeveloped and is now 'The Meadows' residential complex. There is a plaque commemorating the men who died on 16th April, 1941, fixed outside the new building overlooking a memorial garden. In 1940, Mitcham Common was thought to be large enough to have been a landing area for an airborne assault. It was, therefore, defended by barrage balloons, large poles cemented into the ground, and an anti-aircraft gun battery of 3.7 inch guns situated on the south side of the Common west of the Carshalton Road near to the railway line.

There was plenty of aerial activity over London at this time and Mitcham was not spared its share of raids. As a 16-year-old, I would stand on the Common, my tin hat at a rakish angle, and watch in awe as the search lights stabbed the blackness for enemy aircraft. Mostly they only lit up the cloud cover. The glow to the East directed our gaze in search of the enemy who would attack flying westward following the River Thames as it meandered through central London, Battersea, Fulham, Putney and Barnes. Any aircraft that had not delivered all its ordnance thus far would drop it on South London as they fled to the safety of the Channel. Mitcham was beneath their escape flight path.

The Home Guard carried out exercises on the Common mostly without firearms or ammunition. In the early days a broom handle or similar sufficed as our offensive equipment, whilst everywhere we carried the one piece of equipment we would never use; our gas mask.

Knowing that on reaching the age of 18, I would be old enough to fight for King and Country and be conscripted into an arm of the Services, yet still too young to marry or vote, I anticipated the brown envelope from the War Office and took myself down to the recruitment centre in Croydon. This was on 31st December 1942. I was assigned to the Middlesex Regiment. Because so many territorials and volunteers where allocated to the Middlesex Regiment, the 7th Battalion to which I was assigned was split into two, the 1st/7th and the 2nd/7th Battalions. I was in the former. The two battalions were never to fight in the same theatre of war throughout the time I served the 1st/7th.

Within two weeks of signing on, my welding and Home Guard days were behind me and I was instructed to report to Tidworth Barracks in Wiltshire to start my 'square bashing' and basic army training. This was quite a shock to me. I was, for the first time, separated from the safety, assurance and familiarity of home. I was left in the company of strangers and doing the bidding of our trainers who were determined to 'knock some sense' into us and make men of us as well as soldiers. Some of the N.C.O.s we encountered were fearsome mentors whilst others tended to a more paternalistic approach in recognition of our tender years and naivety. It was, however, very difficult and harsh from time to time. Despite this, I achieved the standards required of me. I found the physical demands on my small and youthful frame especially hard. Yet simultaneously I experienced for the first time the close camaraderie of these strangers. The demands placed upon us under training evoked empathy amongst us 'rookies' and we worked for each other to overcome the trials placed before us. We came to laugh at hardship and became philosophical about mistakes. Better to make them here under training than in the heat of combat. I learned about army humour – bawdy, brash, sometimes cruel, yet always inventive. Humour acted as our safety valve in times of stress. And I learned some new words!

The Machine Gunner's Song sheds some light on this:

> *Oh, I'll never forget the day I enlisted on the spree*
> *To be a greasy gunner in a machine gun battery.*
> *My heart is aching, my hands a'shaking:*
> *Sergeant's barking, our souls a'quaking.*

During these six weeks I became fitter and stronger. I learned how to salute, who to salute, and when to salute. I learned how to clean anything – floors with wax polish, windows with Brasso, webbing with waxy goo from a tin and a rifle with a pull-through.

I was given my own little territory, my 'bed space' six feet by four feet. This is the size of a cell in some early prisons! I had the use of a small locker for all my worldly possessions. It was only ever half full. I solved the problem of shining the toe cap of my issue boots so successfully I could see my own reflection on it. Spit is the secret ingredient, mixed with shoe polish. We had lots of time on our hands during basic training so your webbing, bed space and boots would always be immaculate until the R.S.M. or his Corporal decided something was not quite up to par.

We constructed a bed pack to match our bed space. All who have served will recognise that a good bed pack makes a good soldier. Our bed pack – blankets and sheets folded into a neat box shape – always had particular attention paid to it on kit inspection rounds. In order that your bed pack was 'squared off', and so that it would keep in shape during the day, cardboard spacers were discreetly placed inside the pack. In this way crisp corners to the pack could be fashioned. A sagging curve in the pack would develop if such reinforcements were not used.

"We don't want a saggy, baggy bed pack, now, do we?" intoned the duty N.C.O.

Ironing was another skill to be mastered. We were issued with a housewife and a button stick. A housewife was the term for a needle and thread to sew on buttons or insignia, and the latter a gadget for protecting your uniform from polish whilst shining the buttons after sewing them on.

Reveille was at 07:00, followed by a 'flag wag'; a formal parade lasting perhaps ten minutes when the daily raising of the unit flag was witnessed. A welcome breakfast followed. Thereafter, it was all hands to the cleaning and polishing of the barrack room. Floors shone, taps gleamed, sinks sparkled. Next, our platoon would march to huts for lessons on service protocol and tradition, small arms handling and servicing, precautions to adhere to when on the firing range, and a host of other aspects to being a useful member of a machine gun regiment. We became used to being organised throughout each day and in this way the time passed quickly.

After six weeks of initial training I was handed a travel warrant to go to Saighton, near Chester. Saighton Barracks was a large training camp for potential machine gunners. We were to become proficient in the aiming, firing, stripping, reassembly and maintenance of Lewis, Vickers and Bren guns. The training course lasted for one month and was strictly timetabled. We had to be able to perform some of these tasks irrespective of weather conditions. Regrettably, war does not take place in the classroom. You have only to recall the fierce constraints placed upon gunners in the field in conditions of a Siberian winter.

Think of the Battle for Stalingrad from August 1942 to February 1943.

Machine guns can become jammed whilst firing, thus being rendered useless. Barrels have to be changed periodically, especially if they have overheated and water jackets replenished. In conditions as may be encountered in cold climes, these tasks must be performed whilst wearing mittens or similar clothing in order to counter the likelihood of your hand becoming frozen to the metal barrel or other part of the equipment.

The following song, sung to the tune of 'Loch Lomond', illustrates the view of being a machine gunner. It is one of many such ditties composed largely anonymously by serving soldiers of the day:

> *Oh, I'll take the tripod*
> *And you take the barrel,*
> *And you'll be in action afore me*
>
> *And if you get shot*
> *Then I'll have the sodding lot*
> *And I'll eat your rations in the mornee.*

Saighton Barracks was one of two machine gun training camps. Number 26 Machine Gun Training Centre (Saighton, Chester) was formed from the Northumberland Fusiliers and the Middlesex Regiment. Number 24 Machine Gun Training Centre was also near to Chester at The Dale. Depots of the Cheshire Regiment and the Manchester Regiment were trained at The Dale. These centres were established to make machine gunners specialist infantry men. I was introduced to many new skills; machine gun handling was extended to mortarman training, range taking and some new weaponry, the operation and maintenance of Universal Carriers that were to equip Mobile Machine Gun Platoons. The principal weaponry we used was to be the Vickers gun.

Saighton Camp no longer exists. Much of it has been built upon with only a few dilapidated huts remaining of the original 33 hectare camp. The many hours of training, laughter and hard studying are lost in a welter of modern houses. The laughter now is that of children, the training is confined to the school, and the hard studying is in front of a computer screen. Training at Saighton complete, I was transferred to a much older barracks – Fulwood, near Preston.

Arriving there I stopped to admire the imposing entrance. It imitated the grand entrance to a Victorian Gaol.

Main gate, Fulwood Barracks, Preston

"Wow!" I thought. "We're going to prison!"

The main gate approached along a wide drive was an impressive structure, not dissimilar to that of Wormwood Scrubs, but without the white decorative stone. Had there been a drawbridge and portcullis they would not have seemed out of place. The Victorian Gothic style gave a feeling of oppressiveness and permanence. Once inside the massive oak studded gates, all was ordered and regimented. There could be no doubt that these buildings were there to impress. Two squares of barrack block accommodation abutted each other, both two storeys high. They enclosed two large square parade grounds surrounded by a tarmacked pavement wide enough to march a platoon in columns of three. This was indeed a far cry from the randomly scattered concrete and wooden huts of Saighton, separated by large expanses of neatly cropped grass and meandering pathways. The overwhelming feeling that Fulwood Barracks imparted was that, here, we mean business.

Billeted in our designated block, some of us began to explore these new surroundings. To one side stood a three storey building, patently the Officers' Mess, whilst adjacent stood the Senior N.C.O. Mess. We were, however, more intent on finding the N.A.A.F.I., which did not take us very long. All major buildings that served the living requirements of the personnel were within easy reach of each other. Everything had been laid out in a logical manner as a purpose-built establishment that would meet the needs of the Army.

An aerial view of Fulwood Barracks

For us private soldiers, the N.A.A.F.I. was a sanctuary where we could socialise, chat, have a quiet pint and solve all the world's problems in an evening. It was where you learned about the people behind all those new faces. There was humour and teasing, rudeness and carefully concealed blandishment. At times the atmosphere was akin to that of a Northern Working Men's Club. The only women present were serving behind the bar – unlikely and certainly not expected to contribute to the core social activity for which the N.A.A.F.I. Mess was designed in a male-dominated training camp. This was a man's world, although many of those there, like myself, were little more than boys and teenagers.

One of the new faces sitting alongside me on one of these evenings early on during our weeks at Fulwood was John Auger, a Devonshire lad whose West Country burr, strange as it was to my ear, fascinated me. We quickly became friends. A friend was invaluable in new surroundings such as ours. You felt less isolated and better protected for having a mate; someone you could trust. As any experienced soldier will tell you, without absolute trust between you and your fellow soldiers then, in the heat of battle at some anonymous future date in some hell-hole dug-out, all would not be well; indeed, all could be lost. Trust would be a vital component in any action in which you might find yourself.

Volunteers were detailed from this new intake of erstwhile machine gunners and required to fill any number of incidental and secondary duties that oiled the wheels of the camp. After our evening's entertainment, John Auger and I found ourselves required to clean the N.A.A.F.I. on a daily basis. We had landed on our feet on this occasion. We would be indoors on a cold winter's night, and we could take our time over these light duties unobserved by some cocksure Lance Jack or pushy Corporal. We could consume tea by the pint, and even enjoy a digestive biscuit or cream cracker, all in the company of two delightful, chirpy Lancashire girls, the same age as ourselves. As secondary duties went, this could not be better. The relaxed atmosphere in the N.A.A.F.I on such occasions cemented our friendship and we became almost inseparable.

Training at Fulwood continued much on the same lines as that with which we were familiar at Saighton. We stripped and reassembled the Vickers machine gun and the Lewis gun. We were shown how to improvise, should parts wear out, become deformed or broken. We practised the tedium of carrying the gun tripod across rough terrain; a painful experience, whilst another body strained to manage the business end of the gun, a third bore ammunition boxes, and a fourth laboured under the weight of the cooling water jacket and water container. This was arduous for a small man such as me, a mere five feet, eight inches, weighing about ten stone. Yet we managed, common purpose lending a hand, encouraged by our N.C.O. mentors. After a day such as described, the first pint in the N.A.A.F.I. bar at 20:00 tasted especially good, and the two Lancashire barmaids seemed even prettier.

Basic gun handling was augmented with theoretical and practical training on such topics as range finding, fields of fire, use of dial sights and constructing defensive dug-out field positions. Dial sights were adjustable discs that could be fixed in position in front of you and lined up with your target area, so that when the gun sight was in line with the dial sight your gun was always aimed at your target. This led to the best use of your position and reduced the wasted rounds that might otherwise be sprayed around to little avail. In short, it made you and your gun more effective.

August 3rd 1943 saw me take the next step both in my training and towards the day when I would be whisked off on a troop ship to an active theatre. My destination was Rhosnegr, Anglesey, where I became a member of Number 307 Holding Battalion, prior to being posted to Number 1 Reserve Battalion, Special Unit 3. I was to be in Anglesey only three weeks. It was as if we were being held in reserve until the War Office could find us something more useful to do. We certainly felt this, but made the most of our new surroundings. Rhosnegr is a Welsh-speaking village on the west coast of Anglesey, blessed with a lovely long beach, now a centre for wind-surfing. It was very close to R.A.F. Valley which, at that time, sent out Sunderland and Catalina flying boats on Atlantic submarine patrol. It seemed to us that we had been sent on a three-week break by the sea before more serious matters would be addressed.

Everyone in the village was friendly. There were Saturday evening social gatherings in the village hall, film shows at R.A.F. Valley, beautiful scenery to take in, a lovely beach that was too dangerous for swimming and an excellent fish and chip shop, run by an Italian lady, where we would enjoy pies, fish straight from the Irish sea, and shellfish fresh from the fishing boats. The war seemed far away whilst at Rhosnegr. By the end of August, events were beginning to move and bring us all closer to the purpose of our enlistment. On 27th August came a posting to Number 307 Holding Battalion (Special Units), and we were on our way to Towyn, North Wales, near to Abergele.

Towyn was a final machine gunner training camp that specialised in the Bren Gun (of Czechoslovakian make, so-called because the makers were established in the Czechoslovakian city of Brno). Towyn was also by the sea. We shared the site with an anti-aircraft gunnery school. There, targets were drogues trailed behind piloted Hawker Henley aircraft or radio controlled Tiger Moth[3] aircraft, which also trailed target drogues. They did not use live rounds.

As Bren gunners, we also learnt how to use the light machine gun to fire on aircraft using a tall tripod and a helper, who supported either the tripod or the soldier using the gun.

Anti-aircraft firing practice at Towyn

The site had a landing strip of no great length. On a day in September, 1943, an American Air Force B17, finding itself hopelessly lost, landed at Towyn airfield. It had flown from North Africa and was probably low on fuel. Sighting a possible landing area, the crew decided to try

---

[3] Known as Queen Bees.

its luck. They had undoubtedly seen the expanse of water ahead, the Irish Sea, and were likely to have thought that this was the Atlantic. Better to have a controlled crash on terra firma than a ditching in the sea. Aircraft make poor floating platforms.

The B17 was a write-off but the crew of ten were unharmed. They all scrambled out safely and it is reported that some were carrying bananas. These must have been the first of their kind in Wales since September, 1939! I was given one by one of the crew, it was delicious.

Using the Bren Gun as an anti-aircraft weapon

Three further months passed. In December 1943 we learned that our Special Unit of the Holding Battalion was to embark on 13th December and to join a convoy of ships bound for North Africa. We were to miss another Christmas at home. Rommel had been back in Germany when the news broke that the Desert Foxes had been seen off by the Desert Rats of Montgomery's Eighth Army. The Sicily landings were beginning, and a beachhead at Salerno was mooted. Yet our destination in our perspective was unsure. We could but speculate as to our role and final deployment.

We had heard of stories about troop ships crossing the Atlantic not arriving at their destination. There were still many U-boats roaming the seas west of Ireland. The Mediterranean was also home to lone submarine raiders and occasional torpedo aircraft attacks. We had read of the loss of the S.S. *Strathallan* late in 1943; a 22,000 ton former passenger liner. On board her were 4,400 servicemen, several hundred nurses and General Eisenhower's Staff Officers. Most were saved but some perished whilst jumping from the decks of the *Strathallan* into the sea. The impact of hitting the water snapped their buoyancy aid upwards, which broke their neck.

All these thoughts and others pervaded our consciousness. I had never been to sea before. My only experience of the sea was paddling on a warm summer's day. This was different. We were mostly more than apprehensive about our next adventure.

December 13th arrived. Our ship lay by the quayside in Liverpool dock. She was the *Nea Hellas*, a Greek ship formerly owned by the General Steam Navigation Company, but requisitioned as a troop carrier in 1941. The *Nea Hellas* had been built in 1922 as a passenger liner of some 17,000 tons. It sat high in the water with a single tall funnel amidships. We soon learned that the *Nea Hellas* had been given the soubriquet 'Nellie Wallace', probably because the two names sounded similar, but whilst ascribing the real name of a well-known Scottish music hall artiste to her, the ship became somewhat more glamorous. Altogether there were 19 merchant ships and 21 escort vessels in the convoy designated K.M.F. 27. Not all escorts travelled with the convoy for the whole distance of the voyage. About half of the naval escorts joined at Algiers *en route* to Port Said, after setting down provisions and personnel in North Africa. Six of the merchantmen in the convoy were troop carriers, in total conveying over 21,500 troops to North Africa, either to Algiers, Oran, or Port Said.

Departing from Liverpool as part of the convoy K.M.F. 27 were five other merchantmen, the *Maloja, Orbita, Otranto, Orontes* and *Scythia*, which joined up with the *Chyebassa, Highland Monarch, Largs Bay, Leopoldville*, a Belgian merchantman, *Pegu II, Perthshire, Sibajak*, a Dutch merchantmen, *Strathaird, Stratheden* and *Tai Shan*, a Norwegian vessel, all of which had sailed from the Clyde a few days earlier. We put into Belfast a day after sailing from Liverpool on 16th December to be joined by S.S. *Port Jackson* before rejoining the main convoy heading north and then west passing Ulster on our port, and so out into the Atlantic and all that that might offer in weather and U-boat activity.

Once on board the *Nea Hellas* we soon realised that the Navy was very much in charge and that we were part of a precious cargo that had to be carefully protected. We wholeheartedly agreed with the latter!

Upon finding our designated deck we were divided into groups of nine who were given a table and sleeping space. From the deck head to the deck itself was about six feet. Within this, three sleeping stations were arranged, one above the other. The topmost position was a hammock. Below this level a second soldier would sleep on the table and below him the deck itself would suffice as a sleeping space. I was allocated the hammock, which I never mastered. Whenever I went to climb into it, I descended very rapidly out of the other side onto the deck as the hammock first rolled me up into a tube before ejecting me downward! The initial embarrassment was palpable. The Naval ratings were expecting this to happen, whilst the 'hammock hangers' provided much hilarity for the other soldiers with their efforts to get into a hammock. I found I could only accomplish this feat aided by a couple of ratings on hand to steady the contraption and to give me a leg up. I had never anticipated having to be put to bed each evening by a couple of sailor boys!

It was cramped, especially since each group had to stow their packs, kitbags and personal belongings in the same space occupied by us, our table and benches. If there were a scuttle (porthole) nearby we were not allowed to open it. Fresh air came at a premium in these overcrowded quarters. By lights out the air would be thick with smoke, becoming stale with body odour and very warm. One thin blanket would suffice whether you were in a hammock, on the table or lying on a mattress on the floor. As our kapok life jacket was to be within our grasp at all times, overnight it became our pillow.

The S.S. Nea Hellas *in war time livery, 1942*

Our bed space allocated, we all attended a detailed briefing about our ship's dos and don'ts, emergency procedures, inspections, duties and the like. Briefing was rapid fire. Directions to the heads and galley were given. Two men only would collect all the food for everyone at each table in a strict order. Life jackets went where you went. There was to be no smoking on deck at night, but you could volunteer as an extra lookout at night on the upper deck. Your bed space would be inspected daily and your kit was to be stacked neatly, keeping all gangways clear. The list seemed comprehensive and endless. It did, however, end with one instruction that we did not wish to hear; where we should assemble were we to have to abandon ship; in name our boat station.

Ropes cast off, we slowly slid away from the quay at Liverpool dock and heard for the first time the slow rhythmic beat as the engines started to vibrate. Liverpool disappeared into the night and we settled down to our own thoughts about what lay ahead. The briefing, lengthy as it was, had given no hint as to our likely destination. There was a hum of speculation in lowered voices during our first evening at sea, but that was all it was; speculation. Yet, imaginings of our likely destination were soon subsumed by a much more urgent need. That most of us had never sailed before soon became apparent as the gentle swell in Liverpool bay seemed like a Force Seven gale. Many of us were soon hanging over the upper deck guard rail, feeding the gulls with our last meal. For many, this seasickness lasted nearly a week.

I was fortunate that my stomach made no protest about the pitching and rolling of the ship. I kept my breakfast to myself!

One young recruit was less fortunate. Even the smell of food caused violent retching, and he would disappear to the heads or upper deck guard rail to disgorge. After a few days of this, he was in a bad way and looked terrible.

During one such episode of violent vomiting, a friendly senior N.C.O. in the Army approached him, put his arm around his shoulder and said, "Never mind, son. But be careful when you feel that rubbery ring piece in your throat; swallow hard. It's your arsehole!"

This bawdy humour brought a loud guffaw and broad grins to the face of those within earshot. The young recruit, unimpressed, darted away to keep his own miserable company. Despite the occasion, this kind of bawdy humour was never far from surfacing.

After the initial shock of the cramped sleeping conditions, the claustrophobic fug that you met below decks, and the seasickness, we settled into a daily routine. After ablutions, breakfast and bed space inspections we would assemble for boat drill at 10:00 hours. A head count would be undertaken at your boat station, your life jacket would be checked for damage and correct wearing, until the ship's siren sounded. Thereafter, we were dismissed, upon which I would seek out my mate from Fulwood N.A.A.F.I., John Auger, and swap with him our experiences and conjecture so far.

Out first stop was off Belfast, where we were joined by S.S. *Port Jackson,* alongside which we would steam until 21st December when she set off alone from the main convoy destined for Angra dos Reis near to Rio de Janeiro. The five ships from Liverpool and the one from Belfast rendezvoused north of Ulster, close to Malin Head, with the ten ships that had set course from the Clyde on the same day, 16th December, 1943. We steamed in five columns of four ships with our escorts beyond well out of sight of us. The *Nea Hellas* took up its position in the furthest west column following the lead ship, *The Otranto*, also a troop carrier, ahead of the S.S. *Port Jackson*.

Although the *Nea Hellas* was a large ship, nearly 600 feet long and 70 feet wide, I could find my way around her at night after a few days on board. It was December and once out into the Atlantic the cold winds blowing off the sea discouraged me from wandering onto the upper deck to escape the close atmosphere below, even for a short time. Anyway, I was not going to volunteer to be an extra pair of eyes at night on the upper deck, and smoking was forbidden at night time, although it was allowed during the day.

The low hum and vibrations of her six steam turbine engines became a comforting background noise as we ploughed our way through what to me seemed heavy seas southward across the Bay of Biscay before turning east to enter the Mediterranean through the Straits of Gibraltar. This afforded us our first sighting of land for a week. Here, the *Highland Monarch* and *Leopoldville* detached themselves from the convoy. Some of our escort vessels left us at Gibraltar on 24th December to be replaced by others for the final 36 hours to Algiers and several days to Port Said.

I disembarked at Oran on Christmas Day, 1943, along with the 7th Battalion Middlesex Regiment. Within a day or two we were all to be reassigned to the Cheshires, also a machine gun regiment, with whom I would serve until repatriation.

It was a great relief to us all on board the *Nea Hellas* that there had been no submarine or aerial activity directed at us since our departure on 13th December, although I had heard from time to time distant explosions which I took to mean were our own escort's depth charges being used to intercept U boats further out in the Atlantic. I could not, however, be sure of this as I never glimpsed any of our escorts, even on the horizon, whilst in transit. We were all relieved at our safe arrival in Algeria, which was, for a Christmas Day, very spring like. The town of Oran was crowded with allied troops, army vehicles and little else. Oran bore the many scars of a town that had been fought over. The local people looked scared and half-starved. Welcome to the ravages of war. I took it all in without remark. What piece of wisdom could I offer in order to rationalise what lay before me? How had it come to this? I had no answer or real understanding. Best to move on.

We were marched away, carrying all our kit, to a field on the outskirts of Oran, a few miles from the centre. There we were told, "This is your billet."

We were to sleep alfresco in December in North Africa. By the morning, all our clothing and kit was sodden with the heavy dew. Overnight, the temperature was little above freezing. I wished I were back in the warm claustrophobic fug of the deck on the *Nea Hellas*. This lasted two days and nights, until we picked up our kit, looking rather bedraggled and more like refugees than soldiers of the British Army, and were marched to a proper billet in a proper barracks. Not least were we relieved not to be exposed in a field.

Our stay in North Africa was to be brief. It would be only a week or so before we were off on our travels again, yet another step towards our first action in combat. The vast majority of us were rookies. Everything was new to us. That we were not told where we would 'wash up' did not help our optimism, although it was generally accepted by us that to divulge too much to us was a sensible stance to take by our senior officers.

My stay in Oran did afford me a glimpse of the outcomes of battle. It was on one such excursion through the streets of Oran that an extraordinary coincidence occurred. With my ever-present friend, John Auger and a few others in D Company, we were fortunate to meet some Scottish soldiers who were serving in the 8th Army and who were the battle-hardened Seaforth Highlanders. We chatted a while; they the crusty, cynical survivors of the Africa Campaign; we the fresh-faced, wide-eyed innocents about to lock horns with the might of the Reich somewhere in central Italy. There could not be two more dissimilar groups conversing about what had been and what might be.

A chance remark by one of our Scottish friends caught my ear. John had been asked who we were and had given the enquirer our surnames, and that we were of the Cheshires.

"Well now, isn't that strange. We've got a Hawkins fellow with us in our barracks. Royal Artillery I think." My ears pricked.

"Is his name Ivor?" I enquired.

"Aye, that's him all right. Nice chap too."

How strange I mused, it must be my brother, here in Oran. We were not to meet again until after the cessation of hostilities in May 1945, on home ground back in the familiar and safe surroundings of Mitcham.

It boosted my faith to learn that Ivor had survived all that Rommel could throw at him and had played his part in overcoming the Desert Fox.

We gathered our kit and mustered on the parade ground, to be told that we were to march down to the docks in Oran where an L.S.T.[4] would be awaiting us. We were on our way again in a landing craft for Italy. We sat smiling, smoking, chatting, playing cards or just dozing amongst the boxes of ammunition, equipment, vehicles and sundry other items scattered or neatly piled around us. The buzz of speculation could be heard as the large throbbing diesel engines pushed us through the placid waters of the Mediterranean.

Maybe there would be a chance to taste some of that Italian wine we had heard about… Chianti wasn't it? And how about those olive-skinned Italian girls we would meet…

Such idle and unrealistic thoughts kept my mind free for a while of darker matters that could be looming. I took in these new experiences, and observed everything around me rather like my first day at the 'Big School' when I was 11. Everything was larger than I had anticipated – the sea, the sky, the large number of personnel involved in this great exodus; all exceeded my expectations. I was so small and insignificant by comparison. I was a tiny piece in a huge jigsaw. Where did I fit into all of this? It was not so much as overpowering as just very, very BIG. I was part of all this, being swept along in the tide of time, and impotent to influence my destiny.

---

[4] Landing Ship Tank

Eventually, fatigue overtook my thoughts and I dozed a while, which arrested my philosophical meanderings and gave me peace.

I was roused by a nudge on my shoulder. It was John.

"Dougie, have you any note paper? I want to write home before we beach."

I felt in the top pocket of my tunic where, along with my pay book, I kept a small notebook and pencil. "Here you are, John. Two pages be enough?"

"Yes, fine. Thanks."

I looked at the dark blue notebook. Should I send a letter on potentially the eve of my first action? What was there to say?

I could not say where we were heading; that was classified. I looked again at the rather grubby and dog-eared dark blue notebook and thought, *"Yes, maybe I should write home like so many others had done during this sea crossing. How to begin what could be my last letter home?"*

My first action was ahead of me with no certain outcome. The dread of the unknown was set to be tested. I could not relay such thoughts as these to my parents. The neat rows of blue lines remained unfilled. I pondered. The tyranny of the unwritten page had seized my mind.

Part II:
Into Action

I closed the notebook and tucked it back into my tunic breast pocket. I remembered that, besides my Army pay book there was a photograph – a treasured photograph, now quite creased – of my cricketing hero, Headley Verity, the Yorkshire and England Test cricketer. I knew he was a Captain in the Green Howards. What I did not know at that time was that he had fallen in July 1943, not 20 miles from where we were to land on Italian soil, and was at rest in what would become the Commonwealth Graves Commission Cemetery at Cisterna. I straightened the curled corners of my photograph of Headley Verity. My thoughts turned to lighter moments of the game I loved to play.

"Hey! John. That's Headley Verity, you know. Great cricketer! Great spin bowler! Wish I could bowl like him. 'Cept he's left-arm and I'm orthodox."

John looked at the photograph and nodded. There was no glimmer of recognition in John's eyes. Did he know who he was? Did they even play cricket in Devon? I did not know the answer to either question.

He handed me back my picture and I slid it into my tunic pocket. I stood up to stretch my legs after my doze and glimpsed to the north the limestone cliffs of the Amalfi coast reflecting the afternoon sun. To the west of these cliffs I could make out an island, perhaps Capri or Sorrento? It was stunning to see, wrapped in the strong Mediterranean sunlight. It was peaceful and serene. That our landing on the beaches ahead should be thus was a tempting thought.

"Ten minutes!" yelled the coxswain.

This was the signal for us all to collect our kit and muster along the sides of the L.S.T. prior to hitting the shingle beach and juddering to a halt in a couple of feet of water. We were here. The long lines of soldiers shuffled forward nearer to the ramp which was gently lapped by calm waters. Would future surroundings feel as idyllic as this ever again?

Ahead stretched a wide, sandy beach. This gave way to a line of dunes covered with marram grass. To the right I could make out the mouth of a large river as it spilled its waters into the sea. On the horizon ahead of me I could just see a line of low hills covered with olive trees. But for the sound of the sea lapping against the sides of the L.S.T., all was eerily quiet. There were no raucous gulls wheeling overhead; no sound of other birds; no hum of insects; no sound of anything, save the lapping sea. It was 18th January, 1944.

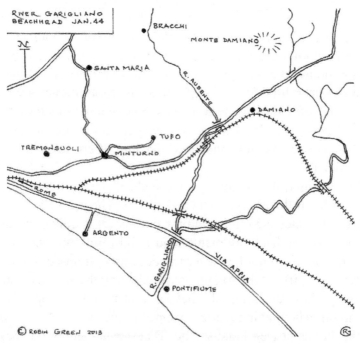

Map of River Garigliano Beachhead

This was two days after the 5th Division, part of Montgomery's 8th Army fighting on the Adriatic coast of Italy, had been moved secretly westwards to the Tyrrhenian coast and positioned north of Naples. The strategy was to force a crossing at two points on the Garigliano River, one centred south of Damiano and the other south of Minturno, and break through the strongly defended Hitler Line positioned in the olive covered hills I had seen on our approach to our landing beach between Argento and the Garigliano Rivers. Such a thrust northwards was aimed at committing General Kesselring's Reserve forces to defend this strong position, so enabling the US 6th Corps to land at Anzio relatively unopposed.

We soon realised the 7th Cheshire Battalion was a reinforcement force for the lower Garigliano River crossing by 5th Division.

The terrain was difficult, being low lying along the coast and affording clear observation by the German defences of Allied deployment, and an unobstructed line of fire from well dug-in positions in the hills south of Minturno. The Garigliano River was about 100 yards wide at its estuary and very fast flowing. Moreover, its banks were steep and in parts the river was deeply incised into the terrain. Thankfully, we did not have this difficult obstacle to overcome under heavy and accurate fire as we had landed on the north side of this estuary. We did, however, receive a warm welcome from the German mortars and artillery. The reality of our reception instantly changed the idyllic view of our landing that I had imagined. I quickly realised why there was no birdsong. Keep your head down and find some cover, any cover, was the order of the day, be it a depression in the beach, a gully in the dunes, or a water-filled trench in the marshes behind the dunes and, at all costs, avoid the mines! Welcome to Italy, and the rigour of the battlefield, my first experience of it.

We set up a position in a large field just inland from our landing area and where it was far drier underfoot than it had been whilst crossing the marshes. The attention we had received by the German gunners was supplemented by the arrival of a flight of ME109s and FW190s, which strafed us whilst alfresco in the fields. The phrase 'sitting ducks' readily came to mind.

To add to our discomfort, we endured torrential rain, which swept in from the west. This was to be one of the wettest Italian winters on record. Notwithstanding our difficulties with the terrain and weather, we made steady progress towards Tufo and Minturno to the north, crossing the Via Appia and Naples–Rome railway *en route*. Fighting was fierce.

> *"The plan of the 5th British Division was to assault across the Garigliano River and advance and seize the high ground on the Tufo feature. Other units (7th Cheshires) were to land from the sea behind the enemy and advance up the coast road. The Garigliano was deep, swift-flowing between high flood banks. The river plain was open with ditches and carrs (to drain the marshes). The Tufo feature was rocky, covered in olive trees, and broken up by dry stone walls with small buildings scattered along the slopes. The German 74th Infantry Division had been in position for several weeks. Dugouts, trenches, wire and obstacles had been constructed... Mines were plentiful..."[5]*

This is how the area in which I was committing my life was described by a regimental diarist at the time of the action. The following text describes the action that occurred over the next few days.

> *"British troops have repulsed two heavy counter-attacks and have advanced to capture the towns of Sui, Tufo, and Argento...* Reuters *reports that the Battle of the Lower Garigliano has developed into a slogging match in which the Germans are slowly getting the worst of it... the ground is thick with mines and is swept by persistent artillery fire machine guns and mortars."[6] (From the German defensive positions).*

The Sappers went in first to clear a route through the densely packed minefields.

---

[5] 2nd Wiltshire Regiment Regimental Journal, December 1958.

[6] *The Examiner*, Launceston, Tasmania 21st January, 1944.

> *"C and D Companies (my company) moved forward but*
> *suffered many casualties in the minefield, the explosions*
> *from which brought down a hail of spurting fire from the*
> *Argento feature..."*[7]

Our training at Saighton, Fulwood and elsewhere had not prepared us for what was, for a battalion of rookies, sheer hell. No training exercise could replicate the intensity of explosions, noise, screams of red-hot jagged shards of metal tearing past our heads. I would hear a dull thud followed by a piercing scream as a comrade nearby was torn apart by this raining shrapnel. A leg would be sliced off here, a head cleft in two over there, a stomach sliced open yonder. What training could have prepared me for this whilst trundling a 30 pound Vickers Gun barrel and wading through heavy marshland in the dark, trying to follow the white tape line laid by our now dwindling force of sappers.

By midday of the following morning we had made little real progress. Our view of our next objective was severely obscured by a heavy mist across the whole of our leading forces caused by the warm sun on the river during a pause in the heavy rain. There was little wind and the cordite from the previous night's barrages hung in the air like a diaphanous shroud enveloping the countryside. We spent the day recovering from our night's exertions; making a brew, warming some bully beef, drying out our socks and similar activities. We were resupplied with water, rations, ordnance, and some man power to fill the evening's losses. Above all, we kept movement and conversation to a minimum as we were very exposed in the low-lying terrain north of the Via Appia, which was overlooked with clear lines of fire from the Natale feature. The ridge that I had seen on our L.S.T. crossing was the same one that we would now be assailing *en route* to Minturno and Tufo. It looked very different now as we slowly and stealthily advanced, carrying our heavy Vickers Gun equipment and supplies. We hugged whatever cover there was available in the knowledge that our every move would be monitored by the German observation posts on the ridge itself. There was a further risk of us being hit by our own

---

[7] George Aris: The Fifth British Division 1939–1945, London, 1959.

artillery as our new forward positions were less than a thousand yards from this ridge, which was the target of our artillery.

We passed Argento on our left and it became clear that the German forces had suffered heavy losses and needed reinforcements before any meaningful counter-attack could be mounted. Our company and battalion commanders urged us on in order to take full advantage of our numerical superiority. These German losses soon became apparent to us as we forged our way upwards towards Tufo and Minturno. In the swirling mists we came across and sometimes stumbled over those German losses, surrounded by spent cartridge cases, ammunition boxes and all the paraphernalia of the battlefront. A thought crossed my mind. With great irony the words "for you ze vor eez ofer" seared itself into my consciousness.

The *Melbourne Argos* reported on 21st January

> *"… progress is painful as the ground is thick with mines and is swept by persistent and accurate machine gun and mortar fire. The British are battling their way yard by yard up a hill (the Natale feature)… Our casualties are not light".*[8]

During these exchanges, sometimes hand to hand with fixed bayonets, many prisoners were taken on both sides. B Company had been reduced to only 40 men whilst A Company had only 31 out of an original 80 or so in each company. As the Natale was *"bristling with enemy machine guns"*[9] we were kept fully stretched and only just held off the concerted German efforts to dislodge us.

We were constantly on the move. A platoon of machine gunners was wanted here; a second platoon was wanted there. Hither and thither we dodged, plugging a hole in the line in one place, lending reinforcing support in another, or giving covering fire for other formations as objectives were seized or hasty escapes were made from areas we were unable to hold. A battle of attrition was taking place.

---

[8] *The Argos*, Melbourne, 21st January, 1944.

[9] George Aris, op cit p.188.

Roman ruins at Minturno where we dug a sangar
amongst the scattered masonry

However, 22nd January saw the landings of the 56th Division under General Lucas take place at Anzio. The principal aim was to make some of the German forces retreat from their defensive positions at Minturno, Castelforte and Tufo, to check the allied landings at Anzio. Aris writes *"it was now confidently expected that the enemy... would withdraw to meet this new threat to Rome... it appeared to make no difference."*[10] A. J. P. Taylor asserts that *"the operation at Anzio, far from aiding the front line in Campagna, broke through and rescued the forces at Anzio."*[11]

I found myself by the end of January defending point 141, the cemetery at Minturno. It was an uncomfortable place to be. Our battalion had lost nearly 200 men; 25% of our strength. We spent our days hidden in our sangar, living on bare slopes and amongst rocky paths. Mules were used to bring our supplies as the heavy rains returned, which turned everywhere but the highest ground or steepest slope into a sea of mud. We were tired, dirty and battle weary, although morale was high amongst the 7th Battalion, so it came as a relief when

[10] George Aris: op cit p.193.

[11] A.J.P. Taylor: "The English Story 1914-1945," page 576.

we heard that we were to be replaced by 15 Brigade on 2nd March. During the quieter times whilst defending point 141, and under cover of darkness, we sent small groups of two or three on patrol to scout the German positions and strength. It was on one of these clandestine sorties that a bakery in Minturno was discovered. To the amazement of everyone, amidst the destruction around them, the family of bakers continued their livelihood, feeding themselves and the other Italian families still remaining in Minturno. The patrol returned safely after one sortie, clutching several loaves of freshly baked bread. The aroma was to die for! This windfall was greatly appreciated by us all. As part of these sorties, the skills I had practised in Mitcham collecting apples from the greenogrocer stood me in good stead. Not a little cunning and subterfuge was required in order to squirrel a few loaves from under the nose of the Italian baker.

The following night a second patrol set off on their scouting mission and returned a few hours later empty-handed. On arrival at the bakery, they had discovered a German patrol doing exactly the same as us. At this juncture, discretion took over and our patrol melted into the night. For some weeks the two opposing armies helped themselves on alternate evenings to the baker's bounty. Each patrol must have known of the other's presence, yet never a word passed between them; this, a parody of war!

Nor was this bakery the only source of extra rations. Another platoon on patrol one evening discovered 'Una Cantina', a vineyard shop that sold its wines direct to the locals. Before a wine tasting could begin, their platoon commander being a wise and cautious man, decided that the wine should be tested. This he did by pouring some onto the floor and placing a lit match to it. It flared into life. The bottle contained not so much fine wine but fine brandy! Thus it was declared fit to drink. That platoon's bully beef was regularly fortified with more than a few drops of the fiery liquid, which would have improved the bully hash immeasurably. So the deprivations and rigours of our stay in Minturno were lightened by these supplements to our diet, and I got to taste the Chianti I had heard of on our Mediterranean crossing. Perhaps the Italian girls would come later.

March 2nd came and went and we were still guarding the gravestones of Minturno cemetery, perched on our rocky outcrops. The irony of this situation must have occurred to one of the platoons' humourists but I do not recall exactly what was said.

Having taken the Natale Ridge, the task was threefold. Firstly, we had to hold what had been won at such a high price. Secondly, after continuous fighting, manoeuvring and fighting again since my arrival in this part of Italy, the order was to recuperate as quickly as possible. Thirdly, we were to continue to harass the German positions whenever the opportunity presented itself. Patrolling, resting, bursts of mortar activity, cleaning, sleeping, eating and routine exchanges with reinforcements became the order of the day.

Demolition explosions could be heard behind enemy lines. This indicated that the enemy might be about to pull out of this sector of the front, perhaps to reinforce their defensive lines at Anzio. Despite skirmishes from time to time, there appeared a more relaxed feeling amongst everyone.

A pigeon race was organised. Lots were drawn to choose a pigeon. First prize, extra N.A.A.F.I. supplies, was won by 'Sarum Sally' who covered the 12 miles to Corps H.Q. in a little over 16 minutes. 'Bit of Brass', King's Own Yorkshire Light Infantry's entrant, finished last. It was claimed that it had been seen dallying with some native pigeons on the way!

By 4th/5th March the withdrawal of Five Division was beginning under our new commander, Major General Gregson-Ellis. I was on my way to Naples where I would rest a while, sightsee and prepare myself and my kit to once more be shipped out for another assignment.

I spent about a week in Naples, during which I visited a grand palace once owned by Italian Royalty, so I was informed. It was like a Renaissance Buckingham Palace surrounded by ornamental Poplar and Cypress trees with Italianate fountains (no longer working) and formal gardens in front and to each side. It was untouched by the ravages of shelling and stood resplendent in sharp contrast to the ruins of the battlefield further north that I had previously encountered; the ruined farm buildings, the shattered village schools and houses, the battered barns and shops that no longer resounded to snorting domesticated animals, playground laughter or village gossip.

About the second week in March 1944, we were given our instructions to once more collect our kit and make our way by army lorry to the quayside in Naples. As part of a reserve division we were being used again to fill a gap, this time at Anzio/Nettuno, some 120 miles to the north.

On this sea trip we were to be transported by DUKW, a much smaller craft designed to carry up to 100 personnel and their equipment close inshore. We passed into the Gulfo Napoli, close to the coast heading westward, leaving the towering Vesuvius behind us silhouetted to the east. We continued between the bay at Pozzuoli and Isola d'Ischia and headed north-west following the Italian coast. Whilst crossing the Gulfo di Gaeta a 'buzz' (rumour) was passed around that our destination would be a ship of the Royal Navy positioned off Anzio, where we were to give added anti-aircraft support fire against the Luftwaffe attacks. I was quite attracted to this idea, as it would afford better protection than that at the front line, the food would be much better, and we would not be sleeping exposed to the elements on board ship.

Twelve hours later we realised that the rumour was just that, and we were preparing to land at the quay in Anzio, now fully functioning as a port after all the mines there had been removed.

On arrival we were greatly cheered by the sound of a band playing 'Swing'. It was quite a large dance band of some 15 musicians. They were very good musicians and one of our troop said that it was Tommy Dorsey's Band. I am not so sure. It certainly lifted our spirits and made us feel welcome and at home, or as close to home as was possible standing on a crowded quayside by a tiny vulnerable beach head.

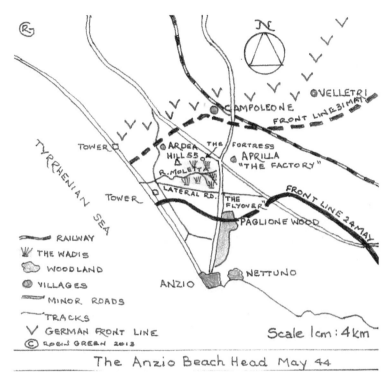

Map of Anzio Beachhead

We crocodiled our way a short distance to a large building close to the quayside railway. Here we were served the familiar N.A.F.F.I meal. It was hot, edible, and there was plenty of it, accompanied by pots of strong sweet tea. The whole meal was altogether much better than that to which we had become accustomed in our sangar at Minturno. Spirits restored, bellies full, we marched away to our billet. This manifested itself as a large, very wet, field on the outskirts of Anzio town. No canvas was in sight. We were to sleep gazing at the stars with but a ground sheet beneath us for protection.

This was still the wettest spring in central Italy on record. Yet, in the Army's time-honoured way, we accepted what was on offer. The concluding feeling was that we could not be accommodated properly – 'There was no room at the Inn' – and that we had arrived unexpectedly!

We endured the night, dozing and trying to keep ourselves dry and reasonably warm. This experience would prove to be a useful training exercise to what, unbeknown to me at this time, lay ahead nine months hence. These uncomfortable and unwelcoming circumstances soon gave way to the real purpose of our presence at Anzio. Within 36 hours of landing we were marching towards the front line, overburdened with our own kit, weapons and supplies. It was very hard going. Passing through our own 'B' Echelon we had glimpses of what lay ahead. There were wooden crosses, simple affairs, dotted around the tented encampment close to our Padre's rudimentary Chapel structure. Nearby was a large tent easily recognised as our medical post by the large red cross in the circular white background, showing clearly on each side of the canvas walls. We smelt enticing aromas from the cook house as we trudged onwards towards the front and were waved to by the large figure of our catering specialist, Alfie Tonks; the man who could work magic with bully or whatever might be available to test his culinary skills.

I was now part of Operation Shingle, the Churchill-inspired strategy to seize Rome.

> *"The Prime Minister had been inspired by a desire to capture Rome and had determined that Shingle would take place and General Eisenhower and General Alexander, without detailed knowledge of the problems involved had agreed to it. Unfortunately... none of those who thus light heartedly decided on the Shingle Operation understood the details of shipping and of loading necessary to put ashore the requisite force and maintain it once ashore."*[12]

---

[12] General Mark Clark's personal diary entry, 2nd January 1944.

Capt. A. L. M. Davis, 7th Battalion padre
at his chapel in the wadis, Anzio

Checking our lines of fire   *Resting up in the wadis*

Machine gun dugout in the   *At La Fossa, the wadis, Anzio*
wadis
Courtesy of Cheshire Military Museum

My lasting impression of the Anzio campaign is one of chaos, disorganisation and lack of purpose, which stemmed from the very senior officers charged with prosecuting the whole operation. I was not alone in this view. All of us Tommies at the coal face had a similar feeling, yet which did not reflect any sense of foreboding. An example of this poor organisation occurred soon after I had pitched my kit at a place where we could construct a dugout, feel protected, yet with clear firing lines of sight. I received an instruction to immediately return to 'B' Echelon, along with several others, to receive our jabs. However, only a few hours before we had passed through 'B' Echelon. In common with all my fellow gunners, I was not best pleased.

We were facing a far superior German force in all respects. There were 20,000 more troops, a superior heavy artillery force, Panzer divisions and machine guns, mortars and the dreaded *Nebelwerfer*. The latter was a fearsome weapon, capable of firing a cluster of ten mortar shells almost simultaneously. It was nicknamed 'The Moaning Minnie' by the Allies because of the sound each shell made as it left the barrel.

Little progress was made during April. A few hundred yards would be gained only to be lost within a few hours by determined counter attacks by the forces facing us, the German 14th Army under the command of General von Mackenson. Elsewhere at 'The Fortress,' a couple of miles east of our position, fighting was even more intense and a frustrating stalemate developed between opposing forces.

On arriving at the front I noticed several curious circumstances. Our lines were very close to the German positions. Indeed, in parts they intermingled. At one time we learnt the Christian names of the Germans immediately in front of us as, each morning, they held a roll call.

"Dieter?"

"Ya."

"Manfred?"

"Ya."

"Johan?"

"Ya."

"Friedrich?"

"Ya." … and so on.

We could hear them chatting, we knew their names, even the names of each of their wives, but we never saw them. In order not to give our position away we were ordered to take a vow of silence. Every little act – stirring your brew, lighting your cigarette, opening a tin of bully – was done with the minimum of noise.

Every night we were entertained by a battalion of frogs serenading each other. Suddenly the frogs would cease croaking; this was the giveaway that Gerry was on patrol very nearby. No one moved or even twitched an eyebrow until the croaking resumed. Then we could relax, a little anyway.

It was soon after our arrival in the wadis that we noticed that smell. It can only be described as the smell of death. Rancid, decomposing German soldiers lay in No Man's Land where they had fallen, sometimes only feet away from our position, and had not been stretchered away or buried *in situ*. Lt. Baker, our Platoon Commander, was so shocked by this that he made representations to his Company Commander that he and a stretcher party could recover and give these men a decent final resting place. This was summarily dismissed by the Major concerned. And so the stench continued, pervading everything; a constant reminder of the inhumanity of war.

I was to take my place alongside my comrades in the sector of the front known as 'the Wadis', a word borrowed from the North Africa campaign. A wadi in North Africa is a wide dry valley. At Anzio, on a much smaller scale, it described the head waters of the Moletta River that flowed east to west, north of Anzio town, rising near to the town of Aprilla. The Moletta had several sources arranged in a dendritic pattern. The area was sandy, covered with thorny scrub, stunted trees and marram grass. Normally these wadis would be dry since they drained very quickly. However, the Sherwood Forester's Regimental Diary of the time describes the area thus:

In the trenches at Anzio.
Courtesy of Cheshire Military Museum

"The drenching rain… had swollen the streams in the bottom of the gully to a deep flood and filled the trenches either side of the streams up to the knee… At night adventurous enemy parachutists crept up to near to the edge of the gully and lobbed grenades into the trenches… By day and night enemy artillery sited on Buon Riposo Ridge directed an unceasing battery of mortar fire and artillery fire onto these trenches. After sunset, more shallow graves would be dug in the sandy soil. Every day the swelling flood would wash away the rough crosses erected to mark the final resting place of a brave soul and wash away the earth from the graves to reveal a khaki-covered arm."[13]

---

[13] Sherwood Forester's Diary, February, 1944.

Or indeed a muddied boot. At this time the Foresters lost 100% of its men and 200%[14] of its officers, a dubious distinction for any British battalion, ever.[15]

Incessantly and remorselessly we were subjected to mortar, *Nebelwerfer* and artillery bombardment at least as intensive as that experienced at The Somme, Passchendaele or Ypres during the Great War. This was augmented by two German monster guns mounted on railway wagons that could fire a round of 200mm calibre a distance of 36 miles. They were on rails that fed into a tunnel in the Alban Hills south-east of Rome itself. Even the Royal Navy ships in Anzio Bay could be targeted by these guns. So the whole of the Anzio beachhead was vulnerable at all times. These guns were affectionately given the soubriquet 'Anzio Annie' and 'Anzio Express' by the Allies. They were not affectionately regarded by us.

In Roman times, Anzio town had been a spa resort. Both Nero and Caligula were born there and regularly visited Anzio where they had palaces to which they could escape the politics and infighting of the ruling classes in Rome at that time.[16] Many of the former Roman buildings that had survived in part up to 1943 were now destroyed by this constant bombardment centred upon Anzio. Parts of the aqueduct still survive, as does the Via Appia, now a six-lane *autostrada*.

Similar actions were taking place at 'The Fortress' and 'The Factory'. At the gully known as Hell's Half Acre the whole of No. 1 Company of the Irish Guards just disappeared. Their fate was learned only when Rome Radio read out the names of some prisoners from this Company.

Captain Raleigh Trevelyan of the Green Howards describes it in this way:

> *"The wadi was full of dead bodies – German, British, American – and all sorts of equipment... The stench of death and cordite was incredible."*[17]

---

[14] All officers killed (mostly to rank of Captain) an all their replacements.

[15] Carlo d'Este. *Fatal Decision*, Arum Press. 2007, p.300.

[16] Caligula A.D. 12–41. Nero A.D. 37–68.

[17] R. Trevelyan. *Rome '44*. Secker and Warburg. 1981, p.156.

Staff Sergeant Bernard Luy was outraged when he encountered several starving pigs, recently escaped from a neighbouring farm, chewing at the limbs of a dead Tommy. Luy shouted at them but his words went unheeded, so, taking his small arm, he fired over the pigs' heads, which had the desired effect and they scattered, probably to feed from another corpse nearby.

"Is this what we are fighting for; to be eaten by pigs?"[18]

In such difficult terrain, all Allied supplies had to be moved under cover of darkness. German patrols could be encountered at any time. So that the muleteers could guide their beasts, lines of white tape were fixed on short poles that led to the Allied forward positions. However, German patrols also ran into these guides, which they would discreetly reposition so that the resuppliers would be led to the German lines. Several groups, along with their mules and supplies, from time to time disappeared without trace. Consequently, the troops missed their meals but, more importantly, risked running out of ammunition and machine gun spares.

I felt that there was no real front line extending from La Cogna in the centre to The Fortress eastwards up to The Factory. Even the hospital, well signed with large red crosses, was shelled on more than one occasion, killing medical personnel and patients.

It was in this mixture of Allied and enemy positions that I first experienced Jerry tanks probing our strengths. There was a constant harassment by both sides. My platoon's position constantly changed as we were forced to move our position and dig in elsewhere, or when we successfully took up more forward locations. We were in the most exposed places and would remain there in the spring rains, unwashed, grimy, smelly and rank for as long as 28 days without relief. Normal bodily functions were a problem, feeding ourselves was a problem, only exceeded by the severe problem that Jerry posed. As a measure of how active our Vickers guns were during the first two weeks of my fighting in the wadis, the three companies of the 7th Battalion,

---

[18] R. Trevelyan. *Rome '44*, quoting Staff Sergeant Luy's actual words.

Cheshires, fired over a million and a half rounds and changed 149 gun barrels. We fought with every kind of machine gun that we could find, borrow or scrounge.

"The 7th Cheshires fought with 56 Vickers, 36 Brownings and as many Brens as we would lay our hands on."[19]

As spring started to show its shoots in early April, as birds began to actively serenade their mates and lay plans for their future amongst the scrubby grass and thorny bushes that were also home to us, I received sad news that our sorcerer with the skillet, Albert Tonks, had been killed. The buzz was that he was extremely unlucky to have caught a piece of shrapnel, or it was a fluke sniper's bullet that found him far from the front at 'B' Echelon. This was exactly a week after my 20th birthday.

My Platoon Commander, Lt C.E. Baker, a volunteer like myself, was a great leader and gentleman. One dark and fearful evening, whilst keeping cave on a German patrol 100 yards away, he noticed my nervousness and called me over to his neighbouring dugout. We chatted. There was nothing special in what he said, yet it calmed me and demonstrated his concern for those, like myself, who were his charges. Everyone always looked out for each other. Lt Baker looked out for all of us in his platoon. He was a cross between an avuncular head teacher and a busy hen protecting her chicks.

There were moments of humour interwoven into the horror of life in the wadis. Jerry sought to weaken our resolve by dropping leaflets suggesting that our loved ones back in Blighty were suffering terribly from the shortages and bombings, or that our wife was giving her attention to another. Such artistic works as the drawing of a women undressing whilst an American stands by over the caption, 'While you die'. Another stated: 'The road to Rome is paved with skulls'.[20]

Some collected these leaflets together and sent them home so that

[19] *Ever Glorious: The Story of the 22nd (Cheshire) Regiment*, Cheshire Military Museum 2009.

[20] G Aris, op.cit, p.224/5

others could share the light heartedness with which we dealt with them. Some were kept as mementoes of the battle, whilst others were stuffed into empty mortar cases and returned to sender. I kept many of these leaflets in my tunic breast pocket as a keepsake. They did not reside there very long.

The Break Out

Operation Wolf was the designated code word for the long-awaited break out. General Mark Clark's solipsistic plan was precipitated by the impending 6th June D-Day landings in Normandy. He wanted two things. Firstly, he wished to 'get in first' before the Normandy landings and secondly, that it would be the Americans led by him who would march into Rome at the head of the Allied forces. Rather than push eastwards or north-eastwards to cut off the German forces from retreating northwards and reforming in other defensive positions, General Mark Clark was intent on the occupation of Rome, an open city, being his primary aim at this time. May 23rd was the date chosen for the initial skirmishes of Operation Wolf of which I was to be in the vanguard as part of 5 Division.

Tons of equipment, ammunition and thousands of personnel were moved forward from reserve positions in the towns of Anzio and Nettuno. I was one of thousands of soldiers. Like a swarm of bees in the May sunset against the blue midday sky, I was hidden by the myriad of others, yet, on close inspection, each one could be picked out in plain view of all the others. And, like the bees, we all worked in unison to achieve the common purpose.

During the subsequent week, D Company advanced to take up positions on the slopes of the Buon Resposto Ridge. Our objective was to secure point 55, a partially wooded and scrub vista that would command an area 2,000 yards northwards and overlook the German positions. It was hard going. The incessant rain of early spring had abated, which facilitated movement across the terrain. However, Jerry was not giving up his territory cheaply. Each small advance was met by determined counter attacks. Having crossed the Moletta River, a small, shallow affair not more than 30 feet wide, we approached the L'Americano, a farmhouse on the north side of the river. A counter attack in the form of a pincer movement held us up. It was only the frenetic engagement of the enemy by the Cheshire machine gunners that eventually caused the counter attack to evaporate with many enemy dead, and many more taken prisoner.

By 27th May, I found myself, along with my comrades, in a new area close to the Anzio/Albano Road in the east of the front near to a position where the Lateral Road crossed over a railway known as The Flyover. We moved cautiously along a road littered with the familiar sight of derelict houses and blackened shells of tanks toward the Buon Resposto Ridge.

As we approached Ardea, resistance by the German forces intensified. A strategy of 'worry and wear-down' was adopted. Yet Jerry was not yielding. My platoon, Number 10, led by Lt C.E. Baker was embedded with the First Green Howards. The strongest enemy positions were stationed on the periphery of Ardea to the east at points 42, 51, 48, 55. The Green Howards attacked these strong points on 31st May and 10 Platoon's role was to consolidate on point 55. It took until 22:00 to accomplish this. During the night we dug in and established a well-screened position close to our forward infantry positions. We were informed that we were to receive tank reinforcements that night. Lt Baker toured all his platoon's positions, speaking to us individually, and was very satisfied with our security.

> "*At 04:15, however, a surprise came. 1st Green Howards and 10 Platoon were counter attacked on point 55 by Mark IV tanks and infantry. The first warning Lt Baker had of the counter attack was the appearance of two enemy tanks camouflaged with foliage from no more than 30 yards away. The tanks fired into the right hand section dugouts at point blank range.*"[21]

---

[21] *Ever Glorious*, op. cit., p.482.

My section, taken completely by surprise and believing that the tanks were ours, could not respond. I stood up and raised my arms. Immediately to my right some ten yards away my good friend, John Auger, and his comrades faced a second Mark IV. It continued to move towards them until it was sitting on top of their dugout. John died at that moment beneath the tracks of a 40 ton mobile gun. I have to this day a vivid memory of my immediate thoughts.

"I didn't expect that."

John was gone, and for a second time I had lost my best friend. I was barely 20.

In all, ten of us were taken prisoner, of whom three later escaped to rejoin their Company.

"Schnell! Schnell!" barked a fresh-faced German soldier. He looked nervous and was about the same age as myself. He was waving his *Mauser* towards the rear of the tank, only ten yards away from where I stood, in order to reinforce his command and indicate to me where he wanted me to go. He grabbed my arm to hurry me along and prodded my rear with his rifle butt. He did not want to be caught in the open, bringing an ignominious end to his moment of triumph by capturing me. I was going to acquiesce with any order he might give me – that is, provided I understood it!

I was stunned at what I had just witnessed. My thoughts were jumbled together as if they had been shaken inside my kaleidoscopic mind. I stumbled along in the dark yet could just make out the outline of a clump of trees silhouetted against the emerging rays of the sun, towards which we headed. I had no inkling what might happen to me in the next few moments, days or months. My thoughts were interrupted by a burst of automatic fire away to my right. I recognised the staccato pulses of a Vickers. The lads were fighting back. Good.

"Schnell!"

Again came the demand to hurry along. I stumbled and almost pitched full length onto my face. Recovering my balance, I half-turned to see what I had tripped upon. I noticed a leg, crooked at the knee and a black uniformed trouser leg with a boot dangling from its end. It was a German boot. Had I done that with my Vickers? I would never know, yet it did give me a certain satisfaction.

We trudged on, now a group of seven with three young German guards, until we reached a small farm building, long abandoned, where we were ordered to stop. It was at this point that a guard noticed my small arm, a Smith and Weston. He indicated that I hand it over. He inspected it, grinned, and slid it beneath his uniform. We were ordered to sit down. It must have been near mid-morning, which meant we had probably travelled ten to 12 miles behind the Gustav Line. It was becoming very warm, warmer than an early June day back in Blighty. We were now very thirsty and one of our group called out in German:

"Vasser, bitte, vasser."

"Nein!" came the peremptory response.

The guards carried water bottles strapped to their waist. We did not. Our water was still in our dugout and the guards were not sharing. One by one we were searched. They were thorough. Those wearing watches had them removed. My tunic pockets were emptied of their contents. I was shocked when my innocent and treasured photograph of Headley Verity was torn into pieces and scattered on the ground. The collection of propaganda leaflets I had assiduously gathered were perused and followed a similar fate. The guard became angry when he saw these. Only my AB61 was handed back to me, my service pay book. Fresh face seemed to know what it was. He must have had a similar document, which he, too, must carry at all times.

Some of the guards smoked. On seeing the 'Senior Service' or 'John Player' packet of cigarettes found on some of my fellow prisoners they smiled.

"Fir gut."

They took one, lit it and handed the remainder back to their owner. This was a token gesture that they were in charge. No one protested. It would serve no purpose to do so and it might anger our captors and goad them into retaliation with a rifle butt jabbed into your ribs.

We rested, sheltering in the shade of the farm building. The searching was over.

"Raus! Raus!"

Why did they always repeat their order? We pulled ourselves to our feet, desperate for a drink, and plodded back into the full glare of the Italian sun. Sweat trickled down our backs. Our faces became streaked with the dust and grime of the battlefield as we wiped away the drips from our forehead and the rivulets coursing down our cheeks. We continued for some hours, hardly noting what we were passing *en route*. Were there people living in this area? We saw no one, but the crops looked tended. Perhaps the locals were more afraid of the German guards than we were and just kept a low profile until we had passed out of sight.

The monotony of this slow march gave me time to think again of what I had witnessed a few hours previously. My mind felt clearer now, but the images were no less sharp. Why had the driver of the tank so close to my dugout stopped, yet that in front of John had not? Clearly, each driver had made a decision; one to stop and menace but not fire; the other to carry on and dispose of the enemy in such a barbaric manner. Both drivers knew that there was nothing that we could do, yet one spared us, and the other felt compelled to enforce his dominant position and save a few rounds from his Spandau at the same time. It was like a metaphor for war. The victor is supreme, the vanquished of no consequence. I would never know the answer to these thoughts. But they assuaged the discomfort of the marching.

After a further hour of shuffling our way through the Italian plain north of the Albano Hills, someone called out, "Hey, lads, how about a song?"

There were dozens of marching songs from which to choose, but the one we knew best was the 'D-Day Dodgers' song.

A tall lad at the front of this sad bedraggled remnant of the 10th Platoon started with the words:

"We are the D-Day Dodgers out in Italy,
Always on the Vino, always on the spree."

One verse, of which there are many, seemed apropos.

"Palermo, and Casino, were taken in our stride,
We did not go to fight there, we just went for the ride.
Anzio, and Sangro are just names,
We only went to look for dames,
For we are the D-Day Dodgers in sunny Italy."[22]

Whilst the singing lifted our spirits, our guards seemed puzzled by it all.

Several hours later, in the heat of the Italian sun, we halted once more. A rocky field lay before us while limestone outcrops were scattered around. There, seated, crouched, stood smoking, dozing or quietly chatting was a much larger group of British soldiers, also P.O.Ws. We joined them, pleased to see our own kind, and rested our weary limbs and sore feet. It was good to take off those issue boots and woollen socks and allow the warm air to circulate between our dusty, sweaty and, I will admit, rather smelly toes.

It soon transpired that our compatriots had been taken at a point further east along the Buon Reposto Ridge and were mostly Green Howards, tough no-nonsense Yorkshiremen for the most part.

We were to stay here the night and would be fed and watered as soon as rations could be found. We were pleased with this. We were all very thirsty and mostly not a little hungry. Still, the company lifted our spirits whilst some claimed that this was far better than dodging mortar shrapnel or rounds from a Spandau or that devilish weapon, the *Nebelwerfer*, our 'Moaning Minnie'. I readily agreed. A further small group joined us towards dusk. Our guards, who had accompanied us thus far, disappeared and new faces arrived to keep order. We each found as comfortable a place on which to lie down as we could and passed the evening smoking and chatting until fatigue overtook our brains and we drifted into a deep slumber. What might tomorrow bring?

I was awakened from my deep sleep by the familiar barked orders. The overnight dew had soaked its way into my bones and a wispy mist was being rapidly burnt off by the early morning sun. With a groan I raised myself to a sitting position. I stretched and rubbed my legs to induce some circulation. On standing up I realised how cold my feet

---

[22] Sung to the tune of 'Lily Marlene'.

were. They were still bare from the previous evening when I had been so keen to allow the air to dry them off from the day's march. I vowed not to repeat this mistake.

It occurred to me that I would by now have been reported missing in action. I did not know how long it would take to pass this information onto my parents and what they would make of it, except that, I knew they would be very concerned and upset and would be praying for me. As it ultimately transpired, but which information I was not to know about for nearly a year, it took until 8th August 1944 for my status as a P.O.W. to be released to my parents – some ten weeks after my capture. It was only through the good offices of the International Red Cross that this kind of information became available to the War Office and hence to the individual family concerned. There were, as I later learned, others who had been less fortunate than I. It was not until very recently that I discovered that a colleague, Private Brass, had perished alongside my good friend, John Auger, during the short action of the evening of 31st May/1st June. A Private Price, who I did not know, had also been mortally wounded at this time.

We continued marching much as the day before, our minds largely sunk in our own private thoughts. I took little notice of where we might be heading or what we passed on the way. I was feeling strangely isolated, uncertain and quite dispirited once I started to realise the magnitude of what had happened to me personally. I felt totally impotent to affect my circumstances and walked onwards to somewhere as if I were on autopilot. I imagined that all of us in that bedraggled group were thinking similar thoughts, buoyed only by the knowledge that we were soldiers, British ones at that, and not ex-soldiers.

Eventually we arrived at a railway siding where a line of enclosed rail trucks awaited us. We sat down beside the rails and each of us was issued with our first rations of the day; one fifth of a loaf of bread, some fish cheese, and a drink. I never discovered what fish cheese actually was. It smelt foul, tasted worse, and as this was all that would be offered nonetheless it went down. I would become very familiar with the fish cheese concoction during the coming months. If only I could have conjured up Albert Tonks, he would soon have turned it into a presentable dish we could enjoy. But he too was in a better place; a place that I also might so easily have visited.

I was ready for a shower to rid myself of the accumulated grime and sweat of the last two days. No such luxury was on offer. Our group of prisoners had swelled to several hundred as, during the day, other groups had joined us from time to time. Some were suffering much more than I, with battle wounds that had not been properly cleaned or dressed. One or two had only one boot. As a consequence they were nursing a lacerated foot from the day's hike.

We were ordered into the cattle trucks, 30 or 40 to each one. A pail had been placed in each one, which we were to share for all our bodily functions. Inside it was airless and very hot. There was little room in which to stretch out so those of us who found a wall against which to lean our back were the lucky ones, able to stretch out our legs. Those in the centre of the wagon had little space in which to relax and had to sit upright with their legs pulled towards their body and their arms wrapped around their knees.

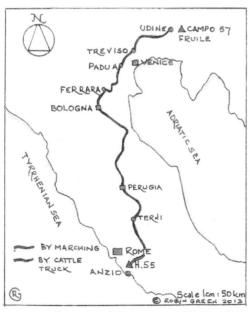

Route from Hill 55 to Campo 57, Fruili

The sliding door was slammed shut and the hasp secured. It was intensely gloomy inside with shafts of light through slits cut high up in the side walls affording some light that illuminated those opposite these ventilation holes. No one said very much. We heard the doors of other trucks sliding into place, followed by an authoritative voice, presumably checking that all were aboard and locked in. Five minutes later the wagon jolted forward. Dry bearings in the wheels grated, metal against metal, as we slowly gained speed. Destined for who knows where. As the sun began to set, the gloom within our little world and in our spirits intensified. Soon I could not see those who sat five feet away from me unless a match were lit by one of the smokers amongst us. The clackety-clack of the wheels as the train travelled over the joints in the rail told of the distance passed. It seemed like the tick of a large clock but in largo time. And in that cattle truck time did pass but slowly. That first night was the longest yet of my 20 years.

We were trundled through the Italian Apennines; we snaked through narrow valleys; we passed through tunnels defined by the change in the pitch of the iron wheels running along iron rails and under high peaks of limestone. The tedium of the journey soon gave way to a nausea caused by the stench emanating from the pail situated in the far corner of the truck, which was now reaching capacity. Small rivulets of dark liquid started to run across the wagon floor as the swaying vehicle slopped unmentionable globules of excreta and urine over the rim of the pail. It seemed an interminable time before we slowed and finally screeched and juddered to a stop in a siding outside a large town that we learned was called Terni.

The wagon door was unlocked and drawn open by a burly, sour-looking German guard. He didn't seem to be very happy in his role as *posten*.

"Out!" he barked in English. We were pleased to escape the fetid, claustrophobic place and gulp in the much cooler night time air.

"Bringen Sie den Eimer mit."[23]

He had now reverted to his native tongue, not knowing how to say this in English. We stumbled out of the wagon door and stood there like

---

[23] Translates as 'Bring the bucket with you.'

recalcitrant teenagers, unsure what was next expected. A welcome drink of what seemed like hot soup was handed out to us all. I gulped mine down in the hope that it would wash away the unpleasant taste I had in my mouth. Fifteen minutes later we were all back in our familiar places inside the wagon. The empty pail was replaced. The door closed and once more I was alone with my inner thoughts and deepest doubts. The next part of this journey was going to be another long pause in my life.

And so the tedious hours passed, marked by the steady clackety-clack of the wheels. The smell and darkness was only punctuated by infrequent stops. Buckets emptied, we returned to our cage and set off once more. At one of these stops a brave soul spied a stream cascading down a narrow gully by the side of the track. Dashing towards it, he was on the point of splashing the mountain water over his face, and no doubt planned to take in a few gulps of its freshness. His attempt was cut short by a sharp thwack across his shoulders as a guard swung his rifle butt at him. He was knocked sprawling and pitched forward into the stream face down. Stunned, he rose and abandoned his quest. We felt sorry for him but could not intervene. I turned away and clambered aboard the wagon. All of us had thereby learned a sharp lesson. A bash from the Boche[24] is not a good idea!

We passed through Perugia, Bologna, and Padua, places that I remembered from my school days learning Geography. There were other sizeable places through which we passed, but of which I did not know. In all, I reckoned we were travelling in that stinking wagon for four or five days until we reached our destination at a place called Udine. It must be in the far north of Italy as that was the direction in which I had worked out that we were travelling. More soup awaited us, more fish cheese, and small lumps of bread were handed out. I wolfed it down. I noticed that some of the group put some of their ration into their pocket for later. However, I believed in now. Later might not come. A column of very old Italian Army trucks was waiting. We were summarily ordered on board and once more set off to somewhere. The violently swaying lorry made a change from the cattle truck, as the lorry was not covered so we could see the countryside about us. We could suck in the crisp

[24] French-Alsace nickname for a German.

north Italian air. Being small, I could slip into a corner of the bed of the truck and stay relatively safe from being pitched over the side by the swaying. Others had to hang on for dear life to stay on board.

"I've paid good money for rides like this at the fairground on Mitcham Common when I was ten or 11," I mused. Now it was free, but I might not like the journey's end!

A couple of hours of this brought us to a large gated compound. Twelve-feet-high wire walls surrounded it. There was a sentry post on either side, each manned by two German guards. Two tall wooden towers stood at the near corners of this compound, equipped with search lights and sirens. There were two or three guards on each tower. The whole occupied a wide, flat stretch of land maybe equal to the size of four football pitches. There were other structures beyond this that I could not clearly discern. Beyond the wire fencing were neat rows of single storey huts, some 40 feet long and 15 feet wide. There were other huts adjacent to these but smaller. Groups of men in uniform stood around or sat on the dusty earth. I recognised the uniform as that belonging to Australian or New Zealand forces. Some turned to gaze at us, temporarily distracted from their game of cards or chess. We were not of any special interest to them as no doubt they had seen it all before. There would be plenty of time later on to greet us and get to know us.

Main entrance at P.G. 57, Fruili, northern Italy

Our guards assembled us into small groups and marched us off to a series of huts set aside from the main regimented lines of huts. We were to be interrogated, disinfected, deloused, showered and given our P.O.W. number. So this was the end of my journey, PG57, Fruili; at least, so far.

The Chapel at Fruili built by ANZAC prisoners of war 1941 onwards. Recently restored

It was now mid-summer and although we were almost as far north in Italy as we could be, it was very warm indeed, which allowed us to wear the minimum of clothing during the day. This enabled us to spend time repairing damage to our clothes, and of course to thoroughly clean them, ridding us of the accumulated vermin with which we had been infested *en route*. We caught up on our sleep too. Food was served on a regular basis and, although not my natural choice of diet, was better than that we had received from our guards. Here, at Fruili, we benefited from a portion of the Red Cross parcels.

The Australian and New Zealand prisoners at Fruili had all been taken in North Africa during that campaign under General Wavell or General Montgomery. Many had been there over a year and so knew the ropes. They were a very enterprising group, having made many escape tunnels with some escapees having success. They also built a wonderful stone chapel, small inside but with a very imposing façade. I marvelled at how this was achieved. The interior was set out exactly as one would have expected it to be, with rows of handmade pews overlooked by a large draped altar decorated with candle holders. The Australian and New Zealanders had achieved all of this during their incarceration. It was amazing.[25] These antipodeans seemed very brazen to me and rather brusque, especially the Australians, but we all rubbed together quite well until the day came when we were told to pack up our meagre possessions and board another rickety truck to be taken to Udini station. From there we embarked upon a similar, yet longer, trip crowded into wagons equipped with only the most basic facilities. We settled down to endure the next phase of our travels.

Again, our destination and route were unknown. Many guessed that we would be bound for a German P.O.W. camp in Saxony or Bavaria or even Poland. For us, all we could do was wait, try not to be noticed, and hope that our destination was in the western part of Germany. We knew that the Normandy landings had taken place, as the Aussies at Fruili had homemade crystal set receivers. Were we eventually to wash up at a Stalag in the west of Germany it was more likely that when the Allied advance reached us we would be repatriated at an earlier date than if we were in a camp further East. Time only would tell us the answer to this.

The train taking us somewhere took about two weeks to reach our destination at Moosberg. I can recall no part of that journey, save that the routine was just as before during our transit through Italy. The same unbearable claustrophobic gloom was endured each day, accompanied by the now familiar primitive toileting arrangements, the near starvation diet, and the raging thirst. Orders were barked and responded to. The guards were sullen, whilst some seemed intent on confrontation in order to vent their own frustration with their circumstances on one of us. We were wiser now and endeavoured to allow them no excuse to show us their rifle butt. We were not in control of our circumstances, yet we learned to manage them.

---

[25] The Chapel still stands to this day and is visited annually by many tourists.

Finally, our trucks shuddered to a halt as we arrived at Moosberg, a vast complex of camps all linked that occupied a site so large its extent could not be seen from ground level.

Stalag VIIA Moosberg main gate which I transited en route   *Roll call at Moosberg, Lamsdorf*

The familiar process of disembarkation, searching, registration and allocation of a billet was repeated. We soon learnt that Moosberg was a vast transit camp, although it did house permanently a substantial number of P.O.W.s. There were many Americans there as well as British, Commonwealth, Polish, Russian, Greek soldiers and some civilians from other countries. In all there were some 30,000 internees at Moosberg. Each nationality had its own compound within the main compound, the Russian being by far the largest.

I was allotted a bunk in a wooden hut similar to those at Fruili, very close to the perimeter fence. Beyond the fence was a wide track that ran parallel to the perimeter with another perimeter fence on its far side. This we soon learned was where the Russian P.O.W.s were billeted. They were treated much more harshly than us. They stood about in tatters, grimy, unshaven and appeared very thin and gaunt.

One evening, the guards sent in their Alsatian dogs, no doubt with the intention of terrorising the Russians. The dogs were released amongst them. Our Russian Allies appeared to welcome this unexpected largesse. There was much yelping and snarling to be heard. Next morning, the guards approached the Russian compound to be met by the sight of their beloved Alsatians' pelts hanging from the wire perimeter. I do not think the Russians debated amongst themselves how best to prepare and serve them. They had certainly welcomed and enjoyed with relish the miscalculation of the guards by releasing the dogs on them. The guards did not repeat their error.

Again, I stayed but a few days in this cosmopolitan camp metropolis. I had just mastered the routine and geography of my own compound when we were marshalled for a third train journey. During the past month I had been on more train excursions and travelled further than at any time in my life. Regrettably, it was not to be Brighton or Eastbourne at the end of the line. Lambinowice, changed to Lamsdorf after Germany overran Poland, Stalag 344, was to be our final destination in an area called Upper Silesia. I wish I had taken more notice of my geography teacher whilst at school. I might at least have heard of the whereabouts of these places, or at least in which country they were to be found.

We travelled eastwards for many days. The tedious and repetitious food, cramped conditions and stifling heat of the journey was only relieved on a couple of occasions when we were attacked by Allied aircraft. American P.51s strafed anything that moved on road or rail. The train would suddenly grind to a halt when attacked. The guards would shout orders to each other, none of which made any sense to me. We were never offloaded from the trains during an attack. These attacks would last for five minutes or so until the P.51s found some other target and broke off, when order would be restored and we could continue. I do not know whether anyone was hurt or killed during these episodes. I suspect some were unlucky. I survived to live another day and reach my destination, Lamsdorf.

Part III: Incarceration

From the siding near Lamsdorf town, Upper Silesia, we were trucked the few remaining miles, glad of the release from that Calcutta Hole called a cattle truck to the gated compound that was Stalag 344. I was again surprised by the extent of this camp. There were two very high perimeter fences, some 30 yards separating each. Tall observation towers were positioned at corners, with others at suitable intervals in between. Shuffling forward towards the outer perimeter fence we were shepherded through and past a small group of six huts – the Straflager, or coolers. On passing through the second set of gates, I was confronted by an extraordinary sight. I turned to my nearest comrade and laughingly exclaimed, "Blimey, mate, we're in luck here. It's full of women!"

Before us cavorted, swaggered and twirled a group of expensively dressed people; dressed in the style of 1920/30 Music Hall entertainers with flowing brightly coloured gowns, flamboyant wigs, and sparkly shoes.

"They're all dancing girls!"

Our exhilaration was soon dashed as I realised, on closer inspection, that the dancers were all blokes in drag, part of one of the many theatre groups of Lamsdorf Camp, out displaying their finery during a Carnival day. What a disappointment this was but, at the same time, what a reception.

We all had a good laugh at this unexpected sight, which did much to dispel the misery of the past days of confinement in transit from Moosberg.

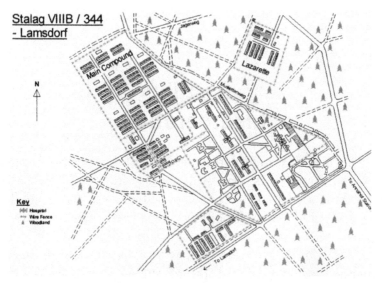

Stalag 334 Lamsdorf camp layout

The 'girls' welcomed us, slapped us on the back and joked about what we had just witnessed. I was led away for processing, registration, delousing again, showering and finally for some food and drink. Importantly, as part of this processing, I had a full medical and dental check by one of the camp doctors, Captain McClardy (RAMC). He was to perform sterling work some six months later. He treated any wounds, cared for your injuries and took a great interest in the health and welfare of all with whom he dealt.

I was allocated an anonymous hut, Number 7A, one of dozens neatly set in rows like soldiers on parade. Sergeant Long was in charge of hut 7A.

"Well, lad," he remarked on seeing my youthful face. "I'll see you right and set you up with something right here."

He was referring to the allocation of work places outside and inside the camp, which accommodated some 30,000 prisoners in all, both within this immediate camp and in the many satellite camps (*Arbeitkommandos*) scattered around the countryside, but which all formed part of Stalag 344.

The German word *Arbeitkommandos* was a word understood by the P.O.W.s to refer to the satellite work camps and the P.O.W. workers who were allocated to work in them.

I was shown my bunk, the lower one of a pair, and given a palliasse and two army blankets. There were 12 to 15 pairs of bunks in each hut. It was gloomy inside. Small windows set low in the walls let in little light. In the middle of the hut on the opposite side to my bunk stood a pot-belly stove; our only heating even when there was fuel, but which was not yet in use as it was still August. A large table and chairs completed the furnishings.

I put my few belongings by the side of my bunk and flopped into the palliasse, resting my head on the two blankets. I realised how much the past six weeks of travel by cattle truck and miserable diet had sapped my strength and drained my spirit.

"A few days of rest and I'll be right as rain." I was asleep before I could complete my thoughts.

Stalag 344, formerly Stalag VIIIB, was the largest P.O.W. Camp under German control. It was opened in 1939 to accommodate Polish prisoners from the Blitzkrieg offensive of September in that year. During its time it handled over 100,000 P.O.W.s from many nations. By 1941, a second camp, Stalag VIIIF, was created to house only Russian P.O.W.s. By 1943, it again had become overcrowded and two more camps were built nearby; Stalag VIIIC and Stalag VIIID at Sagan and Teschen respectively. Many of the other Lamsdorf internees were transferred to these two new camps, especially the lower ranks who worked in the *Arbeitkommandos* of which there were more than 700. *Arbeitkommandos* were working parties outside the main camp complex. The soldiers worked in coal mines, chemical factories, quarries, railways, cement works, farming and at other industrial sites processing timber, beet, leather and other products. The I.G. Farben chemical works at Monowice was established in this area in 1943 specifically because of the availability of cheap labour (mostly British P.O.W.s). One of its products[26] was to be used in the extermination camps as part of 'The Final Solution'. Auschwitz was close by. There

---

[26] Zyklon-B (Prussic Acid).

were nine other adjacent compounds to mine, each capable of sleeping 1,440. Some of the huts had other uses. One was turned into a theatre, another converted as a Chapel, whilst others were used as store rooms for Red Cross parcels and sports equipment.

Lamsdorf camp   *The Lazarette (hospital)*

Just beyond the main compound, and separated from it by a short road, stood the Lazarette. This was the camp hospital facility, by far the best of any Stalag. It housed operating theatres, treatment rooms, an X-Ray unit, wards capable of caring for 60 inpatients, sterilising facilities, a pharmacy and dental practice. It was run by Allied surgeons and physicians assisted by paramedics, nursing staff, radiographers and anaesthetists, all captured serving service personnel. It was overseen by a German doctor called Oberst Arzt (Colonel Doctor) who gave free rein to the Allied practitioners. He was technically in charge but never interceded in the clinical aspects of its running. Unless we were admitted as patients, we were never allowed even inside its compound.

Daily at 14:00 a voice on the camp public address system would announce:

"Heir ist ein Sondermeldung."[27]

There would follow a list of German successes, the tonnage of British shipping sunk, the number of British or American aircraft shot down, and like news items. At each separate announcement we would cheer. This totally baffled the Germans. We already knew the state of the war because we had crystal set receivers made from salvaged components

---

[27] A special bulletin.

brought back by the daily exchange of outside working parties and assembled by expert radio technicians in the camp. We also knew that the World Service, 'This is London calling', exaggerated German losses, but our lies were not as blatant as those of the Axis Powers.

On the morning of my first full day at Lamsdorf, Sergeant Long found me and gave me a job within the camp. He explained that, because of my youth and stature, I would become a cleaner in the Officers' Quarters within the camp confines. He realised that working outside the camp at one of the heavy industry or mining sites manned by the P.O.W.s would soon sap my health and strength. I was very grateful for that and so I became a Mrs Mop.

"Can I do you now, Sir?"[28]

My first full day at Lamsdorf also introduced me to the daily routine. My first 'meal' was issued late morning and comprised of thin soup, being mostly water and very short on ingredients. About half a pint was ladled from a *kubel*, a large metal container, into a tin cup or mess tin per man. It tasted of salt and cabbage. A little later a bread ration of about eight ounces was distributed, followed by a few boiled potatoes. It was just about enough to keep body and soul together. We were all constantly hungry and thinking of the next ration. There were no overweight P.O.W.s anywhere in Lamsdorf camp. Red Cross food parcels[29] were always eagerly awaited and any delay in their arrival at camp was a great disappointment. Should you receive a Red Cross parcel you were known as a 'blue-eyed' boy.

Mornings began at around 6.30am, with the order: "*Aufstehen, raus zum Vielappel*," usually delivered by an elderly guard too old for real soldiering. There were always choice responses from us at this rude awakening, especially when it was raining or cold outside, none of which bear repeating here.

We lined up at the large cesspit-type latrine and, having lightened ourselves, we assembled in threes to be counted. This was done by

---

[28] Catchphrase from Wartime comedy programme, ITMA (It's That Man Again).
[29] See Appendix I: Red Cross parcel contents.

Sergeant Long, our Hut Sergeant.

This daily routine was the occasion to listen to the latest 'buzz', largely comprising speculative ideas about developments in the war. Days passed slowly. For many who did not work off-site on the *Arbeitkommandos* there was little else to do other than play cards, chess, Ludo, or similar board games, chat, write letters home, or lie on your bunk, musing about the past or what the future might hold.

For those like me who did not smoke, cigarettes saved from the Red Cross parcels became a valuable bargaining tool and were the established currency of the camp. There were other ways in which to trade. One such scheme was to empty the small tins of coffee supplied by the Red Cross and replenish them with fillings made up from soil, wood chippings or crushed leaves and topped with a thin coating of coffee. These were then exchanged for cigarettes in trades with other nationalities in separate blocks. There were never any complaints about the quality of our coffee!

I soon learned that one way to survive the privations of the camp regime was to be a member of a small group of pals, maybe five or six of you. We would share Red Cross parcels, trade some items as described above, and barter to obtain other things, usually food, which we had decided as a group would be beneficial. Within the group that befriended me was a sapper called Frank Stapleton. We became very good friends. Also with us was a former manager of a washing machine maker whose name I cannot recall. He invented a cooker for the benefit of us all made from a catering-sized food tin, which was placed on a pan that contained the fuel. This was supplied with air propelled along a tube fixed to the fuel pan. By hand turning two metal impellers set either side of the air tube the heat produced could be regulated. It worked a treat and gave us hot food whenever there was fuel available. It would burn anything.

There were other models of cookers made by imaginative and inventive souls within the camp. They varied in size, efficiency and detail of construction. All followed the same pneumatic principle of having an air-fed fire box fitted beneath a container for liquids; a billy or dixie would serve this purpose. Cooker races were held to see which were the best. Some designs had bellows systems to force air into the fire box, whilst others featured impellers rotated by hand with a crank or driven from a geared drive belt, which was turned by a crank. The makers of these contraptions were called 'tin tappers'. Most later designs were smokeless and portable, and were taken by us when we evacuated the camp in January 1945. They proved invaluable for our survival. Anything that we found, stole or scrounged on the march could be sterilised by boiling, which made it much safer and unidentifiable to eat. Some models even had toast racks fitted to the side of the fire box, enhancing their functionality still further and making them dual purpose. Mouldy bread is better sterilised by toasting.

There was no limit to the ingenuity and resourcefulness of the prisoners. Radio receivers were made, simple cameras manufactured, uniforms with insignia tailored, and more interestingly, a spirit still was set up in the roof space of the hut. Yeast was supplied by compliant guards by bartering good quality English cigarettes, especially Senior Service or John Player. Dried fruit, usually prunes or apricots, were used in the fermenting process. When fully operational, the apparatus made a bubbling noise. When guards appeared to search for illicit items we all burst into song, usually German songs, such as Lily Marlene or Silent Night, in order to drown the noise from the still. The guards were always smiling as they left, pleased with our singing and, crucially, none the wiser.

I soon learned that I could attend lessons in any one of several language courses run by interpreters or bilingual prisoners. Mathematics, First Aid, Literature, Book Keeping and many other basic courses were run from inside the camp. Qualifications in a variety of subjects could be obtained and were certificated by War Office mandarins. These courses provided important distractions from humdrum daily activities, helped to maintain a high morale amongst us, and gave us purpose.

From time to time the German Commandant deemed it necessary to infiltrate a block by sending in a 'spy' in order to establish the nature of any prohibited activities that may be taking place. Such interlopers were soon discovered and quickly disappeared, to be found sometime later in the water tower, which supplied the emergency fire-fighting water to the camp. Needless to say, there was never a witness to such acts.

One hilarious incident created a large 'buzz' amongst us. An Italian P.O.W. had in some way greatly annoyed a group of P.O.W.s of another nationality. In revenge, his rations were spiked with a very powerful enema. A short while after eating his spiked meal he was seen dashing to the sitting-down latrine. This latrine was of a simple construction. A large pit, 20 yards long and two yards wide, by five feet deep, was straddled by a long plank, 'the seat', with an equally long pole used as a back rest. Racing up to the latrine he launched himself at the plank, missed, and landed himself in six months' accumulated excrement. This incident became the centre piece of discussion throughout the many compounds for days afterwards. The laughter could probably be heard in Hitler's bunker in Berlin!

With such a large prisoner population, it is not surprising that every known profession, skill or talent was represented in Lamsdorf. One such talent, which arguably contributed most to the ambience of and high morale within the camp, was that which might be broadly described as entertainer.

The Rhythm Boys and amateur theatre group, Lamsdorf 1944.
Courtesy World War II Experience

There were some who had been involved in amateur theatre or who had been Church choristers or had entertained in local village halls or clubs. There were others who wrote sketches about personalities and events in Stalag 344. Spike Milligan was one such sketch writer and comedian in the army who, post-war, became a household name.

There were several camp theatre groups. Between them there was a production performed in the camp theatre each month. Some were full-length plays, others operettas such as Gilbert and Sullivan had written, whilst a third group represented productions written and scored entirely by the inmates of Lamsdorf. Many of these musicians, actors and librettists went on to professional careers in the Performing Arts after 1945. Denholm Elliott is a case in point.

Costumes and wigs were provided by the Red Cross. Sometimes complete musical scores and scripts of plays also arrived by the same means. Scenery and props were made within the camp, but musical instruments were sent courtesy of the Red Cross. Every performance was well-attended, especially the music hall varieties, which were ever popular, the bawdier the better. A frequent invitee would be the Camp Commandant, accompanied by his senior staff, who were often the butt of many a joke or sketch and frequently lampooned. This was an art form that had long existed, especially in cartoons of public servants, Royalty and politicians, and was continued post-war in popular television programmes such as 'The Goon Show radio programme', 'Not the Nine O'clock News', 'The Goodies', 'Monty Python's Flying Circus' and 'It Aint 'arf 'ot Mum!' and others. The camp hierarchy must have enjoyed the shows because they always answered their next invitation. They too would rather have been elsewhere at the time, I am quite sure.

There were several dance bands formed in the camp. One, I recall, was named the 'Silver Crotchets'. Violins, banjos, accordions, trumpets and clarinets were all represented in these bands. Bruce Harris was an accordion player I met and befriended. The Silver Crotchets was an interesting string quintet comprising viola, three violins and pianist. The viola was played by Lance Corporal Charles and Private Robinson was on piano. They had all been at Dunkirk. As bandsman they were designated stretcher bearers, a non-combatant role who bore no arms, that was recognised as such under the Geneva Convention. Contrary to this convention, they were taken prisoner and after a tortuous and exhausting route transiting Europe became internees of Stalag 334, Lamsdorf. They obtained their instruments via a variety of routes; through the Red Cross supply, by bartering their service watch with a compliant guard for an instrument of choice or by swapping a valued item with another P.O.W. from time to time.

The Silver Crotchets were tasked by the Camp Commander to play at other camps and so in the summer of 1943 visited Stalag III (of *Great Escape* fame) to entertain the P.O.W.s and camp's brass! This was far removed from and much better than being pressed to work in an *Arbeitkommando*.

On Christmas Day, 1944, I was invited by some Australian prisoners to join them for their Christmas lunch and festivities. They were a very jolly and boisterous group on this special day and were determined not to allow the constraints of the camp to restrict their celebrations. For some of them it was their second or third Christmas spent in one Stalag or another. For me, it was my first, and as it transpired my only, Christmas in captivity, yet a memorable one. Bawdy songs, Pommie bashing, and discreet imbibing of the illicit hooch that was produced inside Lamsdorf was crowned by an unexpected event. Someone had managed to smuggle into camp some large canisters about the size of a catering can of powdered milk. These canisters had a substantial ringpull on their base. When 'detonated', dozens of Union Flags the size of a postage stamp were fired into the room, filling the whole space. The whole worked as a very large party popper. Each flag fluttered to the floor like a flotilla of flailing butterflies. The impact was quite spectacular and so unexpected. It brought huge smiles to the faces of everyone. No one was going to divulge to me from whence they had come, save to say that they were smuggled. Once again this indicated to me the resourcefulness of the captive soldier. What next; Folies Bergère-style dancing girls?

A variety of activities were always popular. The Canadians played Ice Hockey during the winter. Their rink was a frozen emergency water supply sunk into the ground. Football was a year-round sport. The players, some of whom had been professional pre-war, had their own coloured strip. Pre-eminent amongst them was Arthur Stevens,[30] an ex-Fulham F.C. midfielder and his brother, a goalkeeper, and a former

---

[30] Arthur Stevens made 413 appearances for Fulham from 1943 to 1959 and scored 126 goals. He died in 2007, aged 86.

player from Newcastle United named Roberts.

Cricket was played between different national teams and Test Matches arranged between England, South Africa, Australia and New Zealand.

Warwick Franks has made a detailed study of the cricket played at Stalag 344 during the war years. Arriving in August 1944, I found it well-established and organised with local rules to take account of the reduced playing area. The cricket played was of a high standard and keenly contested between teams that represented the four principal Commonwealth countries that had Test Cricket as a major component of its summer sporting calendar. Cricket was played elsewhere in P.O.W. camps. Lamsdorf Cricket was special in that it was thoroughly organised, and detailed records of all the matches were kept and still exist, forming an important record of one sport that flourished under inauspicious circumstances.[31]

Sporting activities at Lamsdorf.
Courtesy of World War II Experience

---

[31] Franks. W. Cricket in Stalag 344: Charles Sturt University, Bathurst.

Transportation to an   *Inside the camp chapel. The*
Arbeitkommando   *'Joanna' is behind the cabinet*
Courtesy of World War II Experience

In 1943 a triangular tournament between England, Australia and New Zealand took place. Australia triumphed. With the arrival from North Africa of a large contingent of South African P.O.W.s in 1944, which included a Test cricketer called Billy Wade, they had soon organised a team built around their wicket-keeper batsman. The English team was reorganised. New selections were made and thorough preparations for the series of matches to be played between the four representative teams were completed. The pitch had a matting covering woven on a specially constructed loom made by the camp carpenters from string recycled from Red Cross parcels to protect the dusty and pebble-strewn bowling track. Umpires wore white coats on loan from the medical staff in the Lazerette. Equipment was provided by the Red Cross and Y.M.C.A. Each match would be eagerly anticipated and the possible outcome was seen as a chance to wager a few cigarettes, bar of soap, or occasionally a complete Red Cross parcel. Two series were played from July through to September. I witnessed the second series, which England won. This was followed by two matches between composite sides, the ANZACS versus the Rest, which the Rest won.

Being a cricketing aficionado, I watched every ball, every stroke and every umpiring decision with great joy and interest. Even the absurd was appreciated when, in the middle of one match, a German guard wheeled his bicycle across the pitch accompanied by his guard dog, totally oblivious of the players around him. He received a boisterous and very rude welcome from the assembled crowd. His blushes were, however, spared as he understood none of the invective directed as him.

Major contributions in these matches were made by Fred College, a Military Policeman from Renfrew, and an opening bowler who at a later date in 1948 dismissed Keith Miller in an Australian Tour match of that year, Don Bradman's last tour. Fred Cooper and his brother, Edwin, also played an important part in England's matches that I watched. Fred played for Lancashire in 1946 and later with his brother represented Worcestershire between 1947 and 1950. Celso de Freitas played too in these matches, and represented British Guiana (Guyana now) in the 1930s. He was an elegant batsman, with several first class cricket centuries to his name.

All these high class games were widely discussed and provided an important focus, along with the bands, theatre groups and education courses, for the detainees. They contributed to the physical wellbeing of us all, and eased some of the boredom of the P.O.W. existence. They provided structure and became an emblem of normality: a piece of the village green transported to Poland. Furthermore, they provided a cover for many escapees to try their luck.

These matches form the clearest memories of my time incarcerated in Lamsdorf. They have also earned me a few 'jars' in their recounting in the local. It's an ill wind, as they say.

Athletics was represented amongst these sporting activities, with periodic sports days arranged for everyone's enjoyment. The guards always watched these events enthusiastically. They were, however, rather puzzled by cricket, a game that they were unlikely previously to have seen. All the necessary accoutrements and equipment were obtained through the work of the Red Cross. The impact on the lives of the camp inhabitants of all this activity was immense, and was readily recognised by not only the Red Cross, but also Government Ministers and the senior 'Brass' in the Allied Forces military arm.

The resourcefulness of the P.O.W.s was endless. Those returning to camp from their day's work in one of the *Arbeitkommandos* were briefed to bring back any item that they may find or be able to steal whilst outside the camp. There were three criteria that such an item should satisfy: Is it gettable? Is it edible? Is it tradeable? In the autumn, those working outside the fence on farms would gather a variety of vegetable seeds, peas, beans, beetroot, potatoes, and anything that was available. The seeds would then be dried and stored, ready to plant the following spring in one of the camp's many allotments.

Hut 7A was the billet to which I had been allotted. It was close to the firefighters' 'emergency pond' used by the Canadian Ice Hockey players, and was used as an assembly point for workers who went off-site to work. Rations for these workers were carried outside the camp perimeter fence to a horse and cart that would take the rations to those who needed them. Sergeant Long designated me amongst others to carry these rations. They were transported in what I called a wheelless barrow – essentially a large box structure supported on each corner on long poles. This box was carried by four of us in the manner of a Sedan chair. Not only did the box contain daily rations, it also carried, hidden beneath the bread, clothing and other essentials needed for escaping. There were only ever rudimentary checks by guards at the gates. Had they been more thorough, I would have spent a few days along with three others in the punishment block – the cooler – surviving on bread and water. I did not become familiar with the punishment block's interior furnishings.

Besides being the meeting place for the issue of the bread round for *Arbeitkommandos* personnel, Hut 7A was the meeting place for the escape committee, and the hut where counterfeit documents were made and where camp tailors fashioned replica German uniforms and civilian clothes. It was the hub of nearly all the clandestine activities involved with escaping. Everything that happened in Hut 7A was on a need-to-know basis – I was not part of that scene – but I did learn some of the secrets of Hut 7A.

The camp Chapel was a simple converted wooden hut; a place for contemplation, a place of repose. It was furnished with beautifully crafted pine pews, all made in the camp by joiners, cabinet makers and carpenters amongst the prisoners. A large raised altar stood at the east end, draped in a finely woven cloth. Two wooden candlesticks completed the picture. An old, rather out of tune, Joanna stood in a corner to the right of the altar. It was here that I was Confirmed by the camp Padre. I spent many peaceful and quiet hours in this Chapel, a little piece of home cast into the Silesian forest-covered plains in a back water of a war zone. These moments lost in my own thoughts in this tiny chapel were precious to me. I enjoyed the tranquillity and order it brought, if only for an hour, to a disordered and chaotic world that existed outside this haven.

One of the more intriguing activities at Lamsdorf was the use of bees to carry messages, rather like homing pigeons. There were many former bee-keepers among us; people who could handle bees without upsetting them. Tiny paper strips were attached by strands of hair or silk around the thorax and below the wings. Since bumblebees will return to their colony in the ground from up to a mile away, the bees became a covert communication system between compounds.

There were many characters incarcerated with us. Denholm Elliott was noted for his insouciance. He later became a well-known actor in cinema and television. Boxer Wilmot was a large, powerful man, a former circus boxer who carried the scars that testified to this. Jim Sharpe was tall and lean and known as 'Anchor', a nickname given to him in recognition of his steadfastness under fire. Viktor Konyorsky was a Polish freedom fighter, captured when he was a member of the Polish Resistance. He was the most unlikely soldier, being severely scoliotic – a hunchback.

The most bizarre character at Lamsdorf that I met during my seven months there was an Army Private known as 'Happy Harry'. He acquired this soubriquet in recognition of his determination to escape. His attempts occurred almost on a daily basis. He was always caught because his attempts were spontaneous and opportunistic. He would see half a chance and make a dash for it. Once he even tried to pole vault over the 12-foot fence, having never pole vaulted before. All his attempts were doomed to failure. He was sent to the cooler on several occasions but his aspirations were never dampened. Eventually, the guards even joined in the fun of watching his attempts for freedom and stopped putting him into solitary. Happy Harry provided a regular moment of lightheartedness by his antics, and entertained all who witnessed what became humorous side-shows. I never learnt his surname and often wondered whether he made it back to Blighty.

Autumn turned to winter. It was to prove one of the coldest of the century in Central Europe. In December 1944, an airfield close to Stalag 344 was bombed by American aircraft. Some stray bombs fell on a crescent-shaped building on the edge of our compound. Six Canadians were killed by this friendly fire.

Snow was beginning to accumulate and temperatures sank to -20C at night. In the distance we could hear the gunfire of the Russian Artillery to the east. We realised that the war was unravelling for the Axis and that the end could not be far away. This was confirmed to us when, on 22nd January 1945, we were given instructions that we would be evacuating Lamsdorf in an hour.

The reasons for the release of the allied P.O.W.s from January 1945 have never been fully explained. There seems to be no definitive answer provided as a result of reasoned argument or in the discovery of an order from the German leadership.

Several possible scenarios have been advanced for what amounted to a huge logistical operation aimed at moving 300,000 people in mid-winter from many different locations along unsuitable routes through war zones, intermingled with parallel movements of civilians fleeing the advancing Russian forces.

The reasons, so far as I can discern, fell into two groups.

1. A compassionate response to the deteriorating circumstances of the German nation and its internees with the ulterior motive to save the German High Command's own necks: we are not as bad as you think we are.

2. A pragmatic / political motive to:

a) strengthen the hand of the German negotiator ahead of the anticipated cessation of hostilities by way of an amnesty: P.O.W.s would become bargaining chips;

Or

b) to use quasi-and paramilitary personnel as replacements for regular personnel so that the latter could be used to stem the Russian advance from the east: a distant hope;

Or

76

c) to delay the inevitable in order to allow time for the 'New Weaponry' being developed by The Reich to become operational in the meantime, in the hope of affecting the outcome of the war.

There was a genuine fear of the Russians amongst some of the German High Command. A Communist regime was anathema to the Fascist regime of Hitler's Germany. Moreover, there was a long-standing view held in some quarters of the German leadership that the Slavs were inferior to the Aryans. The German High Command might have felt that the Russians would use the P.O.W.s against them, absorb them into the Russian forces, and arm them.

It is difficult to know which of the above proved to be the most persuasive argument that influenced the German decision to evacuate the Stalags. Fear of the Russians was certainly deeply felt throughout the German hierarchy. The decision, moreover, could have been a combination of some or all of the foregoing, which persuaded the High Command to act as it did. Certainly the outcome of their decision was very unsatisfactory, even disastrous for many who were the victims of that decision. And I was one of those victims.

We rapidly packed our few belongings, our toiletries, all of our clothing, our greatcoat if we still possessed one, and our issue blankets. We lined up outside the perimeter fence and set off at about 6pm. We numbered about 4,000, and a further 4,000 would follow on the next day. We set off into the night, the cold air catching our breath and instantly creating vapour trails around our face. Hauptmann Schultz from Lamsdorf was the German officer in charge of my column of evacuees. He was there in the capacity of Abwehr Officer: *"there was only one medical officer with the first column, Captain A. Stallard (R.A.M.C) who was in a shocking state on our arrival at Gorlitz."*[32]

The snow crunched beneath our boots as we trudged slowly across the plains of Upper Silesa. We continued thus for many hours, some falling behind, others slipping over on snow now turned to ice by tramping feet. One or two carts followed behind to pick up the fallen. The guards were as miserable and fearful as we were; although we had

---

[32] Captain T. McClardy (R.A.M.C.): War Crimes Affidavit, 24th August 1945.

the prospect of freedom, theirs was the prospect of a collapsing regime. Some guards pushed their bicycles through the snow, being unable to ride them in such conditions. We knew these guards well, but we would lose them in a day or two for new faces who would be far less caring than our familiar camp guards.

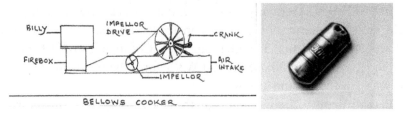

Poston Herzog's lighter gift to me, which still works

We passed through villages lined with women and children – the men were evidently elsewhere – called from their cosy kitchen by the sound of marching feet. They enquired of some of our guards where we were going. I assumed the reply was that we were moving away from the advancing Russian columns. The despair at the sudden realisation of what might be in store was palpable. There were hundreds of thousands who would be cast into the same predicament. The old, the children and the women all feared the Russians more than they feared the German S.S., or the bombing by Allied aircraft. History was to prove that their fears were well-founded.

The first day we travelled some 18 miles and stayed overnight in various barns. There was little room for each individual inside these buildings as more and more were crowded in. Some barns had hay lofts. These soon became as crowded as the areas below. There was no room to pick your way to the outside to relieve yourself, and so those below suffered an unpleasant trickle from above from time to time, as those packed into the hay loft relieved themselves where they squatted. At future overnight stops in barns with hay lofts, there was always a rush to occupy the upper storey after our first night's experience. Later on, I became immune to such discomforts. We all smelt disgusting as our priorities shifted to one of overriding importance; that of survival.

The six of us who had formed ourselves into our friendship group always endeavoured to huddle together and remain as a close-knit group on such occasions. We had our cooker and would pool together the food and fuel we had and share whatever there was available. We all looked out for each other. In this way we all felt that we could come through this enduring hardship.

Within two or three days of the daily task of putting one foot in front of the other, we arrived on the outskirts of a large town called Strzelin. I noticed little as I trudged through the vacant streets, only concerned with the fierce craving inside my belly, the shooting pains in my feet and legs, and the crippling, biting, icy air I pumped into my lungs. My greatcoat collar had small icicles forming along its edge where the vapour from my mouth had condensed. My hands were permanently plunged deep into my pockets in an attempt to stave off the inevitable frostbite. My brain was numb with cold and fatigue, yet with enough spark still left within it to maintain my determination to see this through and taste freedom. How much more of this lay ahead no one knew. I was determined, however, to see another day, and the next, and the one after that. There was little time for conversation. All our thoughts were concentrated into one idea; an over-burgeoning feeling not to succumb.

Yet some were not blessed with such an indomitable spirit. Perhaps they were less well-prepared physically, or maybe were lacking the support and encouragement that I received amid my friendship group. From time to time, we would pass an individual who had slowed for a rest, almost fatal in these exposed conditions, or had fallen in the icy conditions underfoot. Some were helped to their feet and given support and encouragement. Others just lay there by the wayside to be picked up when the column had passed by one of the horse-drawn carts, to be carried to our next destination. This could prove fatal. The loss of stimulation to the limbs would soon take its toll as these parts cooled from lack of movement and hypothermia set in. Many must have perished in this way.

We moved away from Strzelin. There was no let-up in the Siberian weather. I estimated that we were walking 15 to 20 miles on less than 800 calories daily. That was on the days when we actually received any rations. An insipid hot liquid that masqueraded as soup, supplemented with six or eight ounces of bread or *knackebrot,* and a few potatoes, were typical daily rations. An all-consuming thought started to dominate my mind. Food. It occupied my consciousness whilst awake and my dreams whilst asleep. The latter was becoming increasingly difficult as the desire for food and the penetrating cold fought to keep my exhausted mind awake.

A few of us were suffering severely from blistered and bleeding feet by our third day on the road. It was a natural act to remove your boots in order to give some respite or treatment to your feet. It was always a mistake to remove your boots overnight, for by morning they had frozen into harden lumps of leather. It became impossible to lace them up. A pair of iron hard boots flapping about on the ends of your legs exacerbated the sluggish progress you could make.

I did experience a kind gesture on this march from one of the guards that I knew from Lamsdorf. His name was Herzog. We had exhausted our meagre supply of matches to fire up the cooker we had brought with us. Herzog offered me his army issue cigarette lighter, a very sturdy Zippo-type which would not blow out even in a strong wind.[33] Herzog did not smoke so had little use for it. I was delighted as it allowed our group to make a soup of fish cheese, powdered *knackebro*t, some salt and potato peelings that we had found. It was much safer to boil all water before drinking it. Most of the water we used came from melted snow, and boiling it reduced the risk of dysentery and other similar ailments. Some of the soldiers were already showing early signs of that very debilitating condition.

We passed through Jawor, a medium-sized town, trudged slowly through scattered farmsteads and villages, always looking out for any opportunity to steal root crops stored in barns or a chicken scratching a living in the farmyard. Our scavenging excursions were usually undertaken in pairs. Four of us in two groups would steal away from the marchers as they milled around searching for a place in a barn or dispersing among sties, cow sheds or store rooms scattered around the farmyard where they might settle in for the night. We took advantage of

---

[33] I still have this lighter to this day. It is still fully functional.

the confusion that always manifested itself at the end of the day. It was usually very dark. I was small and could conceal myself in the shadowy nooks, wall buttresses or depressions in the terrain more easily than the others in my group. I always enjoyed the rush of excitement that I derived by outwitting the guards that the scavenging escapades gave me. I felt that I had an inner sense that detected danger that I had developed and honed during my childhood pilfering on market day in Mitcham or when I liberated apples from the greengrocers. Mostly we were unlucky, yet the searching did serve a purpose in that it diverted my thoughts from my craving for food, my bodily discomfort, and feeling of intense cold.

Between Jawor and Gorlitz I met with an Australian marcher who had been a cattle rancher working on a huge farm somewhere in Queensland. He would spend days at a time on horseback rounding up cattle prior to them being transported to market. He extolled the virtues of this kind of life; remote, macho and solitary, with only the company of your horse and your fellow ranchers for long periods. Once the round-up was complete and you had been paid for your labour, there followed the mad scramble to spend it all with no cares for the future on drink, raucous behaviour and womanising. As a 20-year-old, some of this lifestyle seemed quite appealing, despite never having ridden a horse before (except a wooden one as a boy at the fairground on Mitcham Common). After all this European nonsense was over, as he explained, I should go to join him in Walliballoo, or whatever this place was called. I said that I would think about it. It all seemed so far away from current circumstances, it was hard to visualise. After that day chatting to him I never saw him again. I wondered whether he made it back to Walliballoo. I shall never know.

From time to time we heard the distant rumble of artillery fire away to our right. My experienced ear told me that it was probably 20 miles or more distant. As night fell on this fourth day, we staggered yet again in to a collection of barns where we claimed our sleeping pitches, the six of us lying together side by side. Once all available space had been occupied, some would take on the role of scrounging and rummaging for food. If caught by the posten would bring instant retribution as I later learned near Meissen. Occasionally we would find discarded vegetable leaves or even a pig swill bin. The latter sometimes gave up small potatoes from its depths, a prize indeed. Anything that could be eaten was seized upon and brought back to the group so that this 'bounty' could be shared.

Three weeks of this hand-to-mouth living and arduous marching brought us to Gorlitz, Stalag VIIIA. We arrived on 5th February, 1945. Gorlitz lies on the border between Poland and Germany on the River Neisse. It is a sizeable town that had a very large Stalag, vacant on our arrival. The former P.O.W.s had been evacuated sometime before. There was clothing, the odd blanket, and some personal items left behind, which the former occupants had been unable to take with them. These things were quickly seized upon by the new arrivals as we filled the vacant huts with our own meagre possessions and sagging bodies. Gorlitz was the location of the execution of most of the 50 recaptured prisoners from the 'Great Escape' from Stalag III.

The accommodation was overflowing with soldiers on the march. There were 7,000 American troops captured during the Battle of the Bulge, many French and a large number of Russians, all of whom were in a much sorrier state than us. The guards we had known in Lamsdorf and who had accompanied us thus far were now replaced. Hilfposten, Volksturm and Abwehr officers replaced them.[34] The Volksturm were a quasi-militia roughly equivalent to our Home Guard, and were generally much older than our Lamsdorf guards. Several *Abwehr*, intelligence officers, were embedded with them along with a *Kreisleiter*, a Nazi Party politico, no doubt present to keep an eye on the others. They were a very unpleasant lot. It was quite evident from the beginning that these new guards would rather have been elsewhere. They soon indicated that they would not tolerate any behaviour that transgressed their rules, which they brutally enforced.[35] Searching for food was fiercely suppressed, and aiding fallen comrades was discouraged by use of a rifle butt or bayonet. Were you Russian, far worse could happen, and did regularly.

---

[34] A British soldier, C. Montaigne states in Q Form, War Crimes Commission affidavit on 31st August 1945. "At Gorlitz, soldier guards were relieved by civilian Volksturm, residents of Gorlitz. They gave us worse treatment than the German soldiers".

[35] See Appendix II: extract from The Geneva Convention.

What the well-dressed long marcher wore.
Courtesy of Cheshire Regiment Military Museum

We remained in Gorlitz for about four days, where we were able to gather some strength and have any medical conditions looked at by one of two Army Doctors walking with us. Captain McClardy, along with Captain Tattersall (RAMC), were ever-present at Gorlitz, patching up, making comfortable and encouraging us with little more than a bottle of aspirin and a box of plasters.

Leaving Gorlitz on 10th February we crossed the River Neisse *en route* to the town of Bautzen. It was somewhere near to this town that we stopped by a farmhouse and, seeing an opportunity, darted off into the nearby farm buildings to see what might be claimed. Our sorties were seen by our guard. We were rounded up and sent to spend the night in a quarry. There was no protection from the elements. It drizzled that night, which not only saturated our outer clothing but also left us shivering and bitterly cold. It was too cold and damp for any of us to catch any sleep that night. I think the punishment affected

Frank more than anyone in our small group as this, in my recollection, was the trigger that started the deterioration in Frank's health. In our weakened state, pneumonia was the great fear foremost amongst us. It was, however, not as deadly as the dysentery that swept through the columns of troops during the coming weeks. Our two doctors carried no medication with them that might alleviate the symptoms or stem its progress through our gut.

Many hundreds were to suffer in this way. The progress of the disease so debilitated the victim that they would be unable to continue. Dehydration and loss of nutrients overcame the body and the spirit. Many fell by the wayside. The Russian prisoners suffered the most – they were the weakest from the outset and usually made slower progress than ourselves. Hence they formed the rear guard of our long column. When they fell by the wayside it was common practice for some of the guards to swiftly and brutally dispose of them.

From time to time our column was joined by others, mostly Russian soldiers. They must have been evacuated from camps in lower Silesia and had joined us from a converging route. Some were mingled in with American, British and other nationalities ahead of me. On approaching a large building one evening I noticed an unusual pile of grey debris lying to the side of the building. As I slowly approached this sight I thought to recognise some of the shapes. On approaching even closer, the shapes resolved into limbs in a limp tangle. There must have been 30 or 40 bodies heaped up – heads lolling, coats flapping, all dressed in the khaki grey of the Russian military. I was shocked and disgusted, yet powerless to act. I wondered, what act of bravado might have brought this upon them; or was this the evidence of fatal brutality dispensed for a minor indiscretion.

Such scenes are supported by data tabulated by Niall Ferguson.[36] The death rate of Russian P.O.W.s held by Germany during the Second World War was 57.5%, which contrasts sharply with the death rate of 3.5% from all causes of British P.O.W.s held by Germany over the same period.

---

[36] Professor Niall Ferguson, MA, D.Phil. He is the Laurence A. Tisch Professor of History at Harvard University: Senior Research Fellow at Jesus College, Oxford: Senior Fellow at the Hoover Institute at Stanford University, USA.

Another disturbing story emerged about the theft of some food from the Luftwaffe at this time by sick marchers, mostly pneumonia, frostbite, and dysentery cases, and two doctors. Captain Tattersall and Captain Clare were treating these sick men. The two Captains were given an hour by the Luftwaffe officers in which to produce the 'stolen' food and the culprits. Failing this, ten men would be shot. They were rescued by two R.A.F. Mustangs making strafing runs over their position, killing 11 and wounding 26. However, the attack did divert the German attention from their loss of rations and they never carried out their ultimatum.[37] But this incident does give an insight into the German psyche.

More random acts of violence were regularly carried out by the *posten* (guards) and *Volksturm* after the exchange of guards at Gorlitz. Many affidavits and special reports were recorded by the Judge Advocate General's staff following the cessation of hostilities, which vividly describe these acts both from the victims' and witnesses' viewpoint. Walter McKibbins records *"systematic brutality by guards towards P.O.W.s by beating with rifle butts, bayonets, fists or feet. These acts ... occurred every day and for no reason except to apparently satisfy sadistic impulses".*[38]

Just looking at a guard could incur a beating, the implement of choice being a bayonet. No facilities for washing or keeping oneself clean, particularly important for those suffering from dysentery, were made available. *"To attempt to obtain water on the march (even for drinking) resulted in blows with rifle butts etc."*[39]

These acts were witnessed by hundreds of men on the march. Better to live dirty than die clean became my new mantra by which to conduct myself. What was somewhat surprising was the insouciance with which these guards behaved. For some marchers, these beatings drained the life forces from an already crumbling spirit and fragile

---

[37] Diary of Captain D.W. Clare (R.A.M.C), January 23rd – February 21st 1945.

[38] Walter McKibbins, ex P.O.W.: 'Form Q': War Crimes Commission, Judge Advocate General's Office.

[39] Walter McKibbins: Op. cit. Ed. Note: About 4.4% of all British P.O.W.s on the various Long Marches died. This is equivalent to roughly 3,500 personnel.

hold that they had on life itself. Good men would be cast aside beyond recovery. These are some of those whose final resting place is unknown. It is my belief that some would have been buried simply in a local family plot or in a wooded area once the column had passed. A simple marker would be placed there but without a name; hidden in plain view.

In an affidavit sworn by Captain McClardy for the War Crimes Commission, he describes the group with whom I marched and which he inspected in Stalag VIIIA in Gorlitz from 5th to 8th February as *"emaciated and in a very distressed condition and suffering from starvation. I examined 50 prisoners who were members of the first party and all were found to be starved and an emaciated condition... they had lost two to three stone in weight"*.[40]

One of the contributing factors for the overriding asthenia of the marchers was the absence of any organisation by the guards to supply basic needs on the scale demanded by the large numbers of P.O.W.s accommodated in Stalag VIIIA. Provision of food was haphazard at best, and mostly non-existent, hence the need for large-scale foraging in the area of Gorlitz by the soldiers, which the guards felt should be suppressed. Even by 10th February, the date on which this march restarted westward from Gorlitz, heading for Bautzen, at least 12 men were reported to have died from starvation alone. As has been noted already, the penalty for foraging was a slap from a rifle butt or bayonet as a deterrent. Besides this, there were at least two reports of soldiers being shot, one fatally.

Two or three guards I noticed who were guilty of this gross cruelty were Unteroffizier Berger, and Stavsgefreite Hertwig. Both joined the column at Gorlitz, ex Stalag VIIIA staff. Their immediate superior officer was Hauptmann A. Schreiber, a former Stalag VIIIA *Abwehr* Officer. He was always distinctively dressed in riding breeches and leather boots decorated with spurs. He was entirely aware of the thuggish actions of his acolytes, Berger and Hertwig, as Captain McClardy pointed in his testimony to Judge Advocate General Officers. No action was ever taken by Hauptmann Schreiber to curb

---

[40] Captain T. McClardy: Affidavit, War Crimes Commission J.A.G Office.

these excesses, despite repeated representations to him by Captain McClardy.[41]

The 'Long March', Jan 1945–April 1945

Witnessing all of this was our small friendship group. Frank was becoming increasingly frail and eventually could not continue. He sat by the roadside in an obtund state, with his spirit visibly crumbling before us; frostbitten, dysenteric, starving, dehydrated and irretrievably weakened. He had been shorn of all dignity, his life was to be forfeited on the altar of 'the Master Race' (*sic*). We attempted to raise him up and support him, carry him if necessary, despite our own enfeebled state. From this we were summarily discouraged by a volley of rifle butts across our shoulders, and so I had to leave my third friend to his awful fate and eventual release from his suffering. We slowly left this scene, I in abject loneliness, slumped, numbed and shuffling away to what lay beyond the next horizon. Another life, amongst so many, had been squandered. Our guards were impervious to this waste; unfeeling and callous. Indeed, it appeared that such impoverished morality was seen by them as emblematic of authority. The view that we can do what we want, how we want and when we want exemplified the vacuity of

---

[41] Hauptmann A. Schreiber was later detained by the Allied Powers at Croutoy-Attichy, France and charged with war crimes. Case No. UK-G/B194, U.N. War Crimes Commission details other indictments occurring at or about the same time; 3rd February – 9th March 1945, and charges a variety of German personnel with contravention of Articles 2, 10, 11, 64 of the Geneva Convention relating to the treatment of P.O.W.s, Hauptmann Schreiber being amongst them. This charge sheet also names Field Marshall W. Keitel and S.S. General Berger, Chief of Staff and Inspector General of Prisoner of War Camps, respectively. See Appendix II.

their human spirit.

Since we had left Gorlitz, all the marchers who had been billeted in the former Stalag there, previously occupied by hundreds of Russian prisoners, had become infested with vermin, lice and fleas. I discovered that the only way to deal with the lice was to put a lit cigarette to them. It was, however, always a battle I was to lose. It was far too cold to disrobe fully in order to reach all the folds and nooks and crannies where the lice could multiply. It was much the same with the fleas who happily jumped from one host to another.

It was at about this time, somewhere *en route* for Meissen (of fine porcelain fame) that I found an opportunity to replace my boots, which were now falling apart. Should this happen there was the certainty of frostbite crippling my feet, which would mean the end of my marching, and the end of me. I spied a fallen dead comrade, unknown to me, by the roadside. I judged that his boots were in a far better condition than mine and of a similar size, so I relieved him of them rapidly. He had no further use for them and this action would aid my survival. It was an easy decision to make at the time, although today it may appear to be grotesque. It was an action borne of extreme circumstance.

I had learned a little about the dreaded frostbite and what it could do to your body if it progressed untreated. An acquaintance of mine, Bruce Harris, who had been an accordion player in one of the bands in Lamsdorf, and having lost his gloves at some point on the march, had been suffering from frostbite in his hands. I had been massaging them daily in order to stem the advancement of this condition. Bruce had found this a very painful experience, but had agreed to it as the only likely treatment in our circumstances. The daily massage had proved unsuccessful and the frostbite had developed into gangrene in two of his fingers. Undaunted, he agreed, despite the severe pain that it caused to massage and bandage his hands with strips of cotton. Bruce bore all his discomfort with great fortitude, survived the march, and returned to playing his accordion. All of this provided a powerful motive for my actions, actions that were repeated many times by other marchers. Sometimes, overcoats, hats, scarves, and even socks were robbed from the fallen. There was always the chance that, were you to be seen by the guards exchanging clothing, a very sharp reminder to desist would be given by the faithful rifle butt!

Between Bautzen and Meissen lies the town of Steudnitz to the north-east of Dresden. It was near this town that a Private Dunn whom I had met received a severe beating for dressing the wounds of a man who had been shot. I have no knowledge of why the shooting occurred. The Bergermeister of Steudnitz was involved in some of the maltreatment of other marchers along with a Kreisleiter called Muller at about the same time. It was about the 12th or 13th of February.

We continued our way, bereft of all dignity, in an almost irretrievably weakened state, driven on by our determination to live whatever it may cost. Yet there remained the inculcated sense that without each other none of us could come through this ordeal. We could not succeed alone. The deep-seated feeling for our fellow sufferers maintained. Whenever the occasion presented itself we did our damnedest to help and support one another.

We passed through Meissen two days after the destruction by allied aircraft of the beautiful medieval city of Dresden. We had heard the aircraft overhead, we had heard the explosions of the ordnance dropped, and we could see the fires still raging a few miles away. The smell of destruction pervaded the air we breathed. Particles of the burning city were sucked into our lungs and made us splutter and cough. It seemed like a metaphor for the whole of The Reich: doomed in the 12th year of its much-heralded 1,000-year reign.

We continued westwards towards Eisenberg, a dwindling band of souls, not recognisable as British soldiers or soldiers of any nation for that matter, and dwindling because increasingly the conditions imposed upon us took their toll. We covered between eight miles and 20 miles each day and arrived at Eisenberg on or about the 20th of February. Food was becoming rarer, small pieces of fish cheese and reduced portions of bread were received on an irregular basis. As we passed through urbanised areas *en route* we were sometimes greeted by locals lining the route, who took pity on us as we trudged and stumbled along. We were offered bread, sometimes drinks and other items of food. The guards would not allow us to accept these offerings and sometimes the women who tried to give us some food would be roughly pushed aside and even struck by an errant rifle butt as reward for their generosity and compassion. Increasingly, our guards were becoming tetchy and nervous as the inevitability of the whole chaotic mess about them was slowly realised.

We were allowed two days of rest at Eisenberg in totally inadequate accommodation, many of us spending the whole time without cover of any sort, irrespective of weather. It was still February, the days were cold and often wet, and the nights freezing with occasional snow flurries. Sitting down was painful, standing up again more so, as our joints and muscles refused to obey our brain. We were rather like a worn out old car engine that had not been run for some time. We, like the engine, could not be fired into immediate life and took a great deal of effort to start. The old engine might have to be scrapped in such conditions. I was not about to allow such a luxury to happen to me!

We left the town of Eisenberg behind us and continued our weary way, alerted from time to time by distant aircraft engines high above, occasionally seeing their contrails and wondering which city in Germany was next on the list for obliteration after Dresden. It was becoming slightly less cold during the day as we were well past mid-February. The nights were still a trial as we curled up wherever we may be in order to catch up on the draining lack of sleep.

One day I noticed that we were approaching a scene I recognised; a scene of high wire fences, tall wooden watch towers and the bleak regimentation of wooden huts stretching as far as the eye could see. On approaching closer, I was shocked to see hundreds of people, all dressed alike in pyjama-style clothing, their tops having alternate dark blue/grey stripes. Their hands clasped the fencing in silent plea, gaunt, barefooted, scrawny and some so weak they defied gravity by standing at all. With no way of knowing who they were, yet still able to be moved by this sight, some of us threw our own meagre bread rations over the fence for them. There was a sudden darting of bodies from all directions such as I had seen only when catfish are fed, as they descended upon our meagre scraps. This was Buchenwald.

Buchenwald camp belied its idyllic name, which translated means

'Beech Forest'. Constructed in 1937, as a concentration camp, it grew to become the largest under the Nazi regime during the Second World War. It took prisoners from throughout Europe and the Soviet Union, as well as the mentally ill, the disabled, Jewish and other persecuted religious orders, Roma, Freemasons and homosexuals, most of whom were used as forced labour in armament factories. The camp's slogan – *Jedem Das Seine* – loosely translates as 'Everyone gets what he deserves,' reflecting the tortured philosophy of the Nazi hierarchy towards the more vulnerable in society. During its lifetime run by the S.S. under Himmler, Buchenwald dealt with a total of 240,000 people, which included a small number of Allied P.O.W.s and a group of between 500 and 1,000 women, some of whom were political prisoners who were later forced into prostitution at the camp. It is estimated that more than 56,000 died within the camp. The primary cause of death at Buchenwald was illness caused by the harsh camp conditions. Malnourishment and hard manual labour took a huge toll of the inmates. Under the policy of *Vernishtung durch Arbeit*[42] the choice was between slave labour and execution. Others died as a consequence of medical experimentation, whilst some were arbitrarily shot or hanged in sadist acts of depravity by S.S. Guards, notably Hauptsharfuhrer Sommer, known as the Hangman of Buchenwald.

I saw these wretched prisoners, not knowing that within a little over a month the American 9th Armoured Infantry Battalion would have overrun Buchenwald camp. A week later, Edward Burrows broadcast these words on CBS News:

"I asked to see one of the barracks. It happened to be occupied by Czechoslovaks. When I entered, men crowded around, tried to lift me to their shoulders. They were too weak. Many of them could not get out of bed. The building, once a stable, housed 1,200 men, five to a bunk. The stink was beyond all description... As I walked out into the courtyard, a man fell dead before me."

42 Translates as 'extermination through labour.'

Burrows continued his visit but would not describe all he saw.

A view in Buchenwald described by Ed Burrows, 1945

We continued our leaden way past Mellingen and towards Gotha. Our guards sensed that there must soon be an end to this fruitless march westward. Their nervousness increased as more and more sightings of Allied aircraft gave the lie to their sense of supremacy. Only the very unobservant or dim-witted could have failed to notice the inevitability of the outcomes of the next few weeks. From time to time, we could hear artillery in the far distance to the west, and that could only mean that it was the Allied guns we could hear.

The nervousness of our guards manifested itself one day as we neared Eisenach.[43] The guards had been chivvying and driving us onwards with their bayonets, rifle butts and dogs. This was by far the worst part of our trek, with rations further reduced to a small daily allowance of knackebrot and a little fish cheese. We were not allowed to assist those who collapsed by the roadside. Were we to attempt to help others, the guards would unleash their dogs on us as further discouragement. None of us was in a fit state to challenge a healthy

---

43 Eisenach was the birthplace of Martin Luther in 1483 and J.S. Bach, the composer, born in 1685.

guard dog, much better fed than we. Another punishment meted out for the smallest transgression of the marching rules was to be tied to a tree or trussed up like a chicken due for market and left in the open for many hours.

We arrived in an area where there were fields of root crops left unharvested. This represented a huge opportunity to us, and the temptation to forage was too great for a small group, among whom was Corporal Pett. Running into a field to collect whatever they could, they were fired upon by some trigger-happy guards as a warning. Corporal Pett was one of several who were hit. He died soon after from his wounds.

We entered Gotha on 4th March 1945, and Eisenach three days later. We had two or three days' rest at Eisenach in a group of former barracks. Captains McClardy, Tattersall and Clare were all kept very busy giving support and treatment to the remnants of the party. All seriously sick prisoners were taken onto a train of trucks, which set off for Bad Orf. A second group, which comprised mostly the senior N.C.O.s, left for Frankfurt to the north. The remainder of the group, including myself, continued westward towards Ziegenhaim. We were a group of perhaps two or three hundred. On this final leg of this hellish marathon we soon approached a large Renaissance building surrounded by high hedges. To the front, a line of tables had been set up. We could make out several nuns, dressed in long black habits, with deep white wimples and a small white bonnet on their head. As we neared the tables I noticed large bowls had been placed in a neat row, piled high with bread. Interspersing these bowls were half-size wooden barrels with brass bindings and leather handles. These were full of steaming broth. What a sight. Such largesse waiting for us, hot and fresh and not a bit of fish cheese in sight. Our excitement was palpable. We waded into this feast, our first real food for nearly ten weeks. At first we could not push this food down our gullets fast enough, yet we soon found that our stomachs had shrunk from the constant small rations to which they were now accustomed. Some of the bread went in to our pockets for another day. The broth warmed us and was full of many different vegetables and a little meat.

One of the Sisters asked us whether any of us needed medical treatment. She was a little taller than me and had the bearing of authority about her. She was in her forties and had kind eyes. When she moved it seemed that she floated, as her feet and legs were completely shrouded by her long trailing black habit. I shyly stepped forward to explain that my piles were becoming increasingly painful. Her expression changed to one of puzzlement. Still embarrassed, I whispered 'haemorrhoids'. Her face immediately changed. She smiled calmly. She spoke almost no English yet the word haemorrhoids was easily understood.

"Kommen Sie here. Folgen Sie mir."

She beckoned me to follow her. We passed through a gap in the hedge along a path which followed the side of the Nunnery and entered through a door marked 'APOTHEKE'.

The room was sparsely furnished with just a small table and chair. A hurricane lamp stood on the table, the walls were lined with terracotta pots of various shapes and sizes, and a large variety of glass jars, either brown or blue or green in colour, each labelled in Latin with their contents, no doubt all herbal remedies. On a shelf above a large white sink were various measuring vessels and two pestle and mortar bowls. She gestured to me to sit down whilst she busied herself for a few moments. She had her back to me, standing by the sink, whilst she mixed some potion in a small jar and dripped an oily liquid into it from a pipette, a few drops at a time. Mixing finished, she turned and presented me with a small jar of a whitish, creamy substance.

"An wended, driemal taglich."[44]

She indicated where I should apply the cream. She smiled and I smiled back, shook her hand and slowly made my way back to the column. I found a quiet spot away from everyone and applied the cream. I felt a soothing glow straightaway. The balm seemed to be a magic potion. I never discovered what it was made from but it was far better than any cream I have used since to ease the discomfort I felt from my piles.

---

44 Translates as 'Use this three times daily'.

The main gate at the Benedictine Nunnery at Fulda
bearing the inscription 'PAX'

I did not know until very recently what order of Nuns had served us such a welcoming feast, or indeed knew the name of the Nunnery we had literally stumbled across. The Nunnery, St Mary's Abbey, is at Fulda near Bad Hersfeld. The Order was a sisterhood of Benedictine Nuns, which had been active in the region since 1626 when the Nunnery was founded. Above the main gate stands a wrought iron archway. Formed within the arch is the single word 'Pax', a singular piece of wisdom when weighed against the preceding five years and the increasing turmoil within The Reich in 1945. The Nuns still maintained a *Biologisher Gartenbau*, producing medicines, ointments and remedies for a variety of ailments. St Mary's Abbey represented an oasis of sanity in my life of the last three months. It is a place that I would really like to revisit, yet I fear the opportunity has now passed with my advancing years. Those Nuns are not forgotten.

We were now in the first week of March and the weather was beginning to improve. Temperatures during the day were now a few degrees above zero, whilst at night time those penetrating Siberian temperatures of a few weeks previously were behind us, although at sunset the frosts returned but were of a lesser severity than hitherto. This improvement in the weather was welcomed by all, yet the principal aim of today was still to see the sunrise tomorrow.

Within a further ten days we arrived at the outskirts of Ziegenhain Stalag IXA, purpose-built as a concentration camp dating from 1939. All manner of prisoners originating from countries throughout Europe were detained here. Russian detainees were subjected to terrible conditions. From 1943, Italian detainees were held here after the capitulation of Italy, whom the S.S. commanders treated as traitors. They were incarcerated with the Russians and subjected to the same awful conditions. Many who entered Ziegenhain Camp did not leave. Russians and Italians were buried in a nearby forest, whilst other western European nationals were interred in a cemetery within the confines of the Lager. Ziegenhain was liberated on 5th April 1945 by a Battalion from the American 3rd Army. It was Good Friday. Over-zealous American soldiers burnt many of the meticulous records the Wermacht had kept since 1939, hence it is impossible to clearly define how many perished whilst at Stalag IXA, of what nationality they were, or how they met their fate.

In 1944, over 50,000 were in Ziegenhain. Most were deployed in *Arbeitkommandos* of which there were nearly 3,000 in the Stalag complex. Francois Mitterand, subsequently President of France, was a P.O.W. at Ziegenhain, having been captured during the first few months of hostilities when he was a national serviceman. He later escaped and made it back to Vichy France where he worked in a junior political capacity.

General view of Stalag IXA, Ziegenhain 1942, and the same camp showing memorial museum 2004

Besides the large number of permanent detainees at Stalag IXA, from April 1944 there were many, like myself, who transited the camp. We were kept separate from the regular prisoners and gained no knowledge of the large numbers held there or of which nationality they were. I was not in any fit state to take much notice of who might be there or even where we were at that time. My body was totally depleted. I had lost a third of my body weight and my brain was hardly registering the time of day, such was my physical and mental state. It was becoming increasingly imperative for me to focus all my remaining energy on being on God's earth for a further day and, with good fortune, the day after that. I was not alone in this trial. Everyone who remained from the original two to three thousand who had left Lamsdorf on 22nd January was in a similar condition, each willing his broken body onwards and hoping that this would be enough to bring to an end this depth of suffering.

We rested a few days here. It is difficult to tell how many rest days we spent at Ziegenhain before once more we were ordered onto the road in our desperate and bewildered condition.

Part IV:
Repatriation

Spring was starting to make itself felt with the absence of night frosts and higher daytime temperatures, which eased the pain of *al fresco* living and sleeping. I awoke one morning in a field and found that we were alone, our guards were gone; overnight they had melted away to leave us to our own fate. It took me some time to realise the significance of this. What we should do, where we should go, in which direction we should proceed, were all questions that confronted us, but answers to which there were none. We stayed where we were, huddled into groups, each discussing the same dilemmas. Some of us soon decided that the immediate option was to set out and forage for food, whilst maintaining a very low profile. We did not know whether our *posten* would soon return to mete out their usual punishments. Time passed and they did not return. Emboldened by this, a small group of us set off to see what we might find. We crossed several fields and soon were alerted to the sound of military transport. Our immediate response was: "They've come back for us."

We scattered in all directions and lay very low, with just one of us keeping cave. The personnel carrier approached. It was evident that we had been spotted and that the carrier was heading directly towards us. As it neared I noticed that the side had an American star on it, rather than the black and white cross of The Reich. The soldiers were in khaki, not S.S. black, and their helmet was quite different from the German helmet. Realisation slowly crept into my addled brain. One of us exclaimed, "They're Yanks!"

This sudden awareness rapidly took hold of us all.

"God! We're safe."

My thoughts tumbled over each other as relief swept through me.

It was the end of a journey. Behind the troop carrier were two large American Dodge trucks, trundling slowly towards us. Each had a high canvas roof, and their powerful diesel engines billowed black smoke from the tall exhaust pipe that stood proudly erect behind the driver's cabin. Emblazoned on each side of the truck's canvas roof were saucy pictures of women, one captioned 'Lucky Lucy' and the other 'Smooth Sue'. These painted emblems were very similar to those painted on the nose of the *Enola Gay* of Hiroshima fame.

Salvation. What a wonderful word had crept into my mind.

"Hey you. Who are you?" These words were said deliberately and slowly.

We were showing no insignia. Why should they know who we were?

"We're British," we called back.

The tension in the American's voice relaxed. "Welcome aboard."

We all ran or stumbled forward toward the truck. A tall American jumped from the truck's cabin and unlatched the tailgate of the nearer truck. We were all laughing. Some had tears of relief and joy mingling with the accumulated sweat and grime of the previous weeks. We shook hands, first with the Americans and then amongst ourselves. One or two could not contain their exuberance and danced as well as they could around the vehicles, whooping and yelling. I had hardly the strength in my body to haul myself onto the bed of the truck. I received a hefty shove from below and was instantly catapulted aboard. All around me as I sat on the bed of the truck I could almost touch the sense of relief amongst us as we stood, sat, squatted or crouched inside the truck, each of us beaming gleefully. I felt a great surge of euphoria sweep through me. Found in plain view.

As two more U.S. Trucks arrived, the first swung away and revved its engine to take us to the American Line. It did not matter that the uneven track rattled us around inside the truck, we were at last heading in the right direction, with friendly faces taking us there. It was the end of the marching rules, the end of the unwarranted attacks on us, and the end of the cruel beatings. It had taken so long to achieve what we now experienced.

A short journey of maybe four or five miles took us to the heart of the American base. Some of us could not climb down from the truck and were lifted down by a group of tall powerful U.S. infantry men. We had all lost so much weight that this proved an easy task for our new found allies. I was led away to a row of trestle tables replete with plates, bowls, billies and mugs, offering ham, eggs, beans, bread, real butter, hash browns and American coffee, made from real roasted coffee beans. I had not seen food like this since on board the *Nea Hellas* which, with all that had happened since leaving her in North Africa 16 months since, seemed like aeons ago. Certainly the U.S. soldier lived better than we had. We all gorged our shrivelled stomachs, which did not take long. The warm rich food inside us took away much of the pain that had been our constant companion. I settled down and was overtaken by deep drowsiness as my body absorbed this sudden infusion of life-saving sustenance. I lay undisturbed for many hours, my body, at last, able to start to catch up on itself.

How many days we stayed with the American 3rd Army is unclear to me. I received every courtesy and consideration whilst I was among them, despite the Americans being engaged in a relentless advance across Bavaria towards Berlin. It was 4th April when we were found by the U.S. soldiers. Ziegenhain was relieved the following day, so we were about to be joined by an estimated 4,000 more ex-Ziegenhain P.O.W.s, about a third of them Americans who had been taken in December of the previous year during the Battle of the Bulge.

After several good meals and some days' proper rest under canvas on comfortable beds, all the British were called to be registered, de-loused and showered before we were scheduled to be flown out by D.C.3 transport aircraft. The American base was stationed on the periphery of an airfield which acted as the supply terminal for 80 Corps. Aircraft arrived with regularity, bringing all manner of ordnance, personnel, food, and other necessities to the Front Line. It was these aircraft, which normally returned empty, save for casualties, which were designated as our transport. We were to be flown to Brussels where a series of repatriation hostels had been set up specifically to handle returning P.O.W.s. It would be my first flight in an aircraft, a week or so after my 21st birthday, which I had forgotten all about, having been otherwise occupied at the time. Repatriation would be enough in itself to celebrate my birthday.

And so we said goodbye to our American rescuers and friends. As we entered the Dakota up a small stepladder we were once again asked to offer our bodies to be sprayed with DDT. Some of the American aircrew had complained about the number of little creatures others had left behind on board. We were still wearing our original uniforms from Lamsdorf days and many of the little beasts had made a home and settled down to bring up their family in the folds of our clothing. I had been sprayed more often than my dad sprayed his greenhouse tomatoes against whitefly during the summers of the 1930s in Mitcham.

I settled back into the parachutist's seat with which the aircraft was fitted. They were uncomfortable and made you sit bolt upright and were aligned on either side of the fuselage, facing each other. We were briefed by one of the aircrew:

"Don't go for a walk outside."

"'Fraid you can't smoke on this aircraft."

That is all I recall from his words. He disappeared forward onto the flight deck and we were on our way, the first stage of our return to Blighty.

We taxied to the end of the active runway, lined up and began to roll as the twin engines were opened up to full throttle. Twenty seconds later we were airborne, passing over the wreckage on our starboard side of a burnt out D.C.3 which had crashed on take-off a couple of days earlier, killing all on board, including some ex-P.O.W.s. As a first-time air traveller this sight was not at all auspicious. I sat in my para-seat and kept my own counsel. I passed the noisy journey thinking about my homecoming in Mitcham, now only weeks away.

The pitch of the aircraft engines changed as the throbbing power was reduced on our descent into Brussels International Airport. Bump, bump, the main wheels hit the runway surface, followed by a second gentler bump as the tail wheel contacted the macadam strip. We were down and safe. On taxiing onto the dispersal area I noticed a small reception group comprising several military ambulances and some buses. I descended the steps onto the hard-standing to be received by a

W.R.A.N.S. Sergeant Nurse, wielding yet another DDT canister. They were surely determined to 'get those critters'.

Settling down on the hard wooden slatted seats of the bus, we knew now that at last we were truly safe and would be cared for and brought back to full health as soon as could be managed. Our reception had a tinge of returning heroes about it. The gathered assembly clapped us as we made our way from our transport. We didn't feel like heroes. We were just bloody tired!

Outside repatriation hostel, Brussels, May 1945

The five-mile bus journey ended in front of a large anonymous 19th Century building in the centre of Brussels on the edge of a cobbled square. Draped above the wide imposing entrance fluttered a banner with the word 'HOSTEL' sewn in large black capital letters. This was where we would stay until arrangements were made for onward transit to the U.K. Everything looked very civilised and low key. We were greeted by half a dozen New Zealanders who were staying there. They smiled and were genuinely pleased to see us, even though we were complete strangers to them.

"You'll enjoy it here," I heard one of them say.

"Clean, crisp sheets and all that," advised another.

I perked up at this, not knowing beforehand what to expect.

I was led through corridors and up several flights of stairs. Everywhere looked a bit run down, which was not surprising since Belgium had just been liberated after five years of occupation. The hotel management must have liked dark green paint. It was to be found everywhere. Yet it did a good job in disguising the scuffs and the finger marks. I was shown a room, MY room, which was simply furnished with a bed, table, two chairs, a lamp, wash bowl and jug of water. Further along the corridor I was shown a vast bathroom with a white tiled floor and blue and white tiled walls. The bath was the biggest I had ever seen and stood raised on lion's claw feet in the centre of the room.

"I'm going to enjoy that," I mused.

It was time to test out the bed. I turned back the counterpane and revealed the lightly starched, gleaming white sheets. I sat on the edge of the bed. It sank beneath my meagre frame and enveloped me in its luxury. I slowly lay back and stretched my arms sideways as if I were floating on water. Closing my eyes to concentrate on the opulence engulfing me, I soon passed into oblivion. Some hours later, refreshed and very hungry, I quickly acquainted myself with the bathroom and then sped down the dark stairwells looking for a place to eat. The dining room was full but a kindly group made room for me at their table. A white damask tablecloth covered the circular table. There was a posy of wild flowers in a small glass vase in the centre of the table. Real shiny cutlery lay arranged before me. A glass jug full of iced water graced the table. This was a far cry from the dirty, freezing and dank places where I had 'dined' during the three preceding months, surrounded by straw, mud or sometimes worse. The contrast between this civilised meal and those of the immediate past was arresting. It was as if too much change was happening in too short a time. It was all very difficult to take in at once. I was soon settling into my soup, proper soup with many bits in it, a far cry from the thin brown liquid we had become accustomed to on our travels. There was little chatter at our table, in fact, the mood was sombre. Was this the result of our unexpected release from deprivation or were we simply concentrating on the fare before us? Another course, this one of pasta (I think), cheese (hurrah!), tomatoes and some other unidentifiable vegetables replaced my soup dish. This too went down, hardly touching the sides of my gullet. Tea was served to complete the meal. I was very full, very warm and very tired. Time now to try out the bath.

I slept well that first night between those crisp white linen sheets. Contentment surrounded me, except I could use a new uniform and some better boots. Breakfast was continental style, fresh croissants, which I had never seen before, and a sort of coffee. Had I asked, I could have had a boiled egg and toast with which I would have felt much more familiar, but I knew that that would keep for another day.

We were given a cigarette ration and spent the mornings exploring the centre of Brussels. I visited the grand Cathedral and saw the Manneken Pis. St Michael's and St Guruda's Cathedral atop the Teurenberg Hill reminded me of Lincoln Cathedral with its two tall towers framing an imposing entrance. The bronze statue of Manneken Pis dating from 1618 was much smaller than I had imagined. That too reminded me of another statue I had read about, the Little Mermaid in Copenhagen. It was refreshing to just wonder where your eye might take you; to stop and gaze with no constraints, no barking *Schieber* lackey at your back and no forced marching. Daffodils were starting to bloom, something I had not seen for some time. They lifted my spirit and gave me a feeling of optimism, a feeling I had not known for nearly two years.

Our days in the hostel in Brussels were lazy days, days of freedom, days of gentle banter when no one mentioned the events of the preceding months. This was no doubt part of the healing process of our shattered bodies and our shattered minds.

Having regained some of my strength with the nutritious regular meals that we all enjoyed, and having cleansed our bodies of the vermin, accumulated grime and sweat of our travels and exertions; having refreshed our tired limbs and scrambled minds, next we were to be shuttled from our hostel in Brussels back to England sometime during the coming weeks. Our rooms would be needed for the next wave of returning P.O.W.s, rescued as the Allies pushed further into Germany from the West.

I stayed in the Brussels hostel for two weeks. By 24th April, the time had come for me to be flown home. We were bussed back to Brussels airport where a 'Stirling' of Bomber Command was waiting. It was a noisy, cold, draughty aircraft, not designed as a troop transporter. Despite this, I was glad to be heading towards home with the prospect of proper hospital care and to meeting with my family once again.

The Stirling landed at Didcot near Oxford. From there I was admitted to a military hospital, probably at Halton near Wendover in Buckinghamshire, although I cannot recall the exact details now. My stay in hospital was quite lengthy. I was not discharged until 20th June 1945, some six weeks after the cessation of hostilities in Europe. I had regained the weight I had lost, nearly one-third of my original body weight, and thrown off the effects of dysentery. The next day a full medical declared me fit to serve again as a regular soldier.

Street party, Mitcham 1945, to celebrate Victory in Europe.
Courtesy Merton Historical Society

There followed a period of leave, the likes of which I had not enjoyed since signing on in December 1943. I recall a grand street party that was held in early August to celebrate V.J. Day held in Mitcham High

Street. Everyone whom I had known from my Home Guard days was there. The weather was glorious and I had lots of fun. I also spent a lot of time answering questions about my war experiences.

I was 21 and had no job to which to return. It seemed sensible to me to take up the Army's offer to remuster and use my welding background in the Royal Electrical and Mechanical Engineers. Training began on 19th August with the South Staffordshires, to be posted later to Harrogate where I worked in a R.E.M.E metal fabricating unit. It was a regular 08:00 to 17:00 job, which left time in the evenings and weekends to play cricket, a game I loved. Harrogate has a Yorkshire County Ground and this is where I met Yorkshire and England all-rounder Maurice Leyland. He was a lovely man and invited me to play at the County Ground in his XI against other top class Yorkshire teams in friendly matches. I was honoured and jumped at this opportunity. The social life after the games was not to be missed. This led to my meeting Mavis, who I later married in September 1946. We took a small stone cottage in Starbottom, a hamlet in the Wharfe Valley in the shadow of Buckden Pike. It was an idyllic place to be. Our nearest neighbours were the sheep on the fells. It was very isolated in winter, which made getting about for shopping and the like quite tricky.

My time in the Army was coming to an end. Although I had been promoted to Corporal, increasingly I felt it was not the life for me or Mavis that I wanted. I resigned from the Army and was discharged in August 1947 and returned to Mitcham to where it all began. Combat – 90% boredom and 10% sheer terror – was behind me forever. Now my life could begin again.

Epilogue

Doug Hawkins recovered from the privations of The Long March and remustered into R.E.M.E as a welder. He married in 1946 and had two children. Whilst stationed near Harrogate he played cricket for Maurice Leyland's XI (Ex. Yorkshire and England Test Cricketer). Doug left the Army in 1947. He now lives in Hampshire.

Leonard Price, 7th Battalion Cheshire Regiment of Ellesmere Port, lies at rest in the Rome War Cemetery. He was taken on 1st June 1944, aged 25.

Captain Headley Verity, Green Howards, was mortally wounded near Caserta on 31st July 1943 and is resting in Caserta War Cemetery. He was aged 38.

John Auger, 7th Battalion Cheshire Regiment from Bantham, Devon, was 24 when taken and rests in the Anzio Beach Head War Cemetery.

James Brass, 7th Battalion Cheshire Regiment from South Shields, was killed on 31st May, aged 21. He rests at the Anzio Beach Head War Cemetery.

Captain Raleigh Trevelyn of the Green Howards survived the war and became a journalist and author.

Albert Tonks, 7th Battalion Cheshire Regiment of Wednesbury, died on 22nd March 1944, from war wounds, aged 35. He rests in Gradara War Cemetery.

Frank Stapleton (sapper), from Leeds, probably died at the roadside near Mellingen around the end of February 1944 from dysentery and exhaustion. I have been unable to trace his final resting place.

Lieutenant C.E. Baker, 10th Platoon Commander, 7th Battalion Cheshire Regiment, survived the war.

Sergeant Long, NCO in charge of Hut 7A at Lamsdorf. Looked after

Dougie by not sending him on *Arbeitkommando* work. Sergeant Long's unit is unknown. He probably survived 'The Long March'.

Captain A.L.M. Davis, Padre 7th Battalion Cheshires. Captain Davis survived the war.

Captain McClardy, Captain Tattersall, Captain Clare (all R.A.M.C) cared for the P.O.W.s especially during the Lamsdorf to Gorlitz part of The Long Walk. Doug Hawkins knew them all. These three doctors had all worked in the Lazerette at Lamsdorf. All survived the March.

'Happy Harry', Lamsdorf internee. So called because of his repeated attempts to escape almost on a daily basis. His rank, unit and surname are unknown to me. I do not know whether he survived the March.

Staff Sergeant Luy, Green Howards survived the war.

Bruce Harris (accordion player), who Dougie helped during The Long March, survived.

Hauptmann A. Schieber, Abwehr Officer from Gorlitz (Stalag VIIIC) was indicted for War Crimes.

Appendix I:
Red Cross parcel contents

- Tin of cocoa powder
- Bar of milk or plain chocolate
- Tinned pudding
- Tin of meat roll
- Tin of processed cheese
- Tin of condensed milk
- Tin of dried eggs
- Tin of sardines or herrings
- Tin of preserve
- Tin of margarine
- Tin of sugar
- Tin of vegetables
- Tin of biscuits
- Bar of soap
- Tin of 50 cigarettes or tobacco (sent separately)
- ¼lb of tea

Appendix II:
Geneva Convention Summary
(pertinent to Prisoners of War)

The third Geneva Convention ('Relative to the Treatment of Prisoners of War') covers members of the Armed Forces who fall into enemy hands. They are in the power of the enemy State, not of the individuals or troops who have captured them.

Prisoners of war MUST be:
- treated humanely with respect for their persons and their honour;
- enabled to inform their next of kin and the Central Prisoners of War Agency (ICRC, the International Red Cross) of their capture;
- allowed to correspond regularly with relatives and to receive relief parcels;
- allowed to keep their clothes, feeding utensils and personal effects;
- supplied with adequate food and clothing;
- provided with quarters not inferior to those of their captor's troops;
- given the medical care their state of health demands;
- paid for any work they do;
- repatriated if certified seriously ill or wounded (but they must not resume active military duties afterwards); and
- quickly released and repatriated when hostilities cease.

Prisoners of war must NOT be:

- compelled to give any information other than their name, age, rank and service number;
- deprived of money or valuables without a receipt (and these must be returned at the time of release);
- given individual privileges other than for reasons of health, sex, age, military rank or professional qualifications;
- held in close confinement except for breaches of the law, although their liberty can be restricted for security reasons; and
- compelled to do military work, nor work which is dangerous, unhealthy or degrading.

Bibliography

Aris G.R.: *The Fifth British Division*. London 1959.

Trevelyn R.: *The Fortress. A diary of Anzio and after*. Buchan and Enwright. London 1985.

Trevelyn R.: *Rome 44*. Coronet Hodder and Stoughton 1983.

D'Este C.: *Fatal Decision*. Aram Press, London 2007.

Page M ed.: *Kiss Me Goodnight Sergeant Major*. Granada, London 1973.

Waite C.: *Survivor of the Long March*. Spellmount, London 2012.

Kemp P.K. Lt Cdr.: *The Middlesex Regiment 1919–1952*. Gale and Polden. Aldershot 1956.

Diary of the Cheshire Regiment 1939–1944: 'Do You Remember' & 'Forever Glorious', self-published.

Merton Historical Society, various newsletters and pamphlets self-published.

WWII Experience Museum, Wetherby: photographic documentation.

Saunders S. ed.: 'The Long March' transcript. ASA Productions 2008.

About the Author

Born near to the Yorkshire Dales, Robin attended Wyggeston Grammar School in Leicester and Birmingham University. There followed a career in the RAF as a Flight Lieutenant Air Navigator until 1971. A second career teaching in primary schools followed where Robin developed an interest in teaching mathematics.

Retiring early, Robin took up bowls which is where he met Doug Hawkins. Following a bowls match they conversed at length where Robin learned some of Doug's background; that he had survived the 'Long March', January 1945 to April 1945, and that Doug had this strong desire to have his story told.

Doug recognised that he did not have the skills to do this himself so he invited Robin to write his story for him. Robin took up the baton and wrote *Lambeth to Lamsdorf*, his second book.

Robin lives in Hampshire in retirement and continues to write.